THE
GOSPEL-SHAPED LIFE

THE
GOSPEL-SHAPED LIFE

Ian Hamilton

THE BANNER OF TRUTH TRUST

THE BANNER OF TRUTH TRUST

3 Murrayfield Road, Edinburgh EH12 6EL, UK
P.O. Box 621, Carlisle, PA 17013, USA

*

© Ian Hamilton 2017

*

ISBN
Print: 978 1 84871 721 3
EPUB: 978 1 84871 722 0
Kindle: 978 1 84871 723 7

*

Typeset in 10/14 pt Sabon Oldstyle Figures at
the Banner of Truth Trust, Edinburgh

Printed in the USA by
Versa Press, Inc.,
East Peoria, IL

*

To my dear friends
in Second Presbyterian Church, Yazoo City,
with thanks to God for your love and
encouragement over many years.

Contents

Introduction

The word 'gospel' means 'good news'. The best-known and perhaps best-loved verse in the Bible admirably captures what this good news is: 'For God so loved the world, that he gave his only Son, that whoever believes in him should not perish but have eternal life' (John 3:16). The gospel is first good news about God ('God so loved the world'). Second, the gospel is good news about a Son given by God to be the Saviour of the world ('that he gave his only Son'). Third, the gospel is good news for a world of judgment-deserving sinners ('that whoever believes in him should not perish but have eternal life'). Sadly, however, many people's understanding of the gospel begins and ends with John 3:16. The gospel is not one iota less than John 3:16; but it is very much more.

It is the purpose of this little book, what the Puritans would have called a *vade mecum* (literally, a 'go with me', a book that would fit easily into a pocket), to explore the multi-faceted character of the gospel and to show how the gospel comes to shape every aspect and detail of our lives.

In Romans 6:17 Paul tells the church in Rome that though they were once 'slaves of sin', they 'have become obedient from the heart to the standard of teaching' to which God had committed them. 'Standard of teaching' could be better translated 'mould of teaching'. What Paul has in mind is the life-shaping influence and power of gospel truth. The gospel not only rescues us from hell and brings us to heaven, it also takes possession of our lives to remake them into the image and likeness of our Saviour, Jesus Christ (Rom. 8:29). This is God's ultimate purpose for all his blood-bought and dearly-loved children. He purposes not only to bring us to heaven, but in doing so to conform us to the likeness of his Son. Jesus is himself the gospel-shaped life.

If there is one thing this book seeks to say it is this: *Jesus Christ is himself the glory and grace of the gospel*. He is the good news that God in his love and grace has given as a free gift to the world (2 Cor. 9:15). This is why the New Testament's most common description of a Christian is someone who is 'in Christ'. It is only in union with Christ that the rich blessings of the gospel become our personal possession. In Ephesians 1:3-14 Paul highlights this foundational truth in a series of 'in Christ' statements. 'In Christ' God the Father has blessed us 'with every spiritual blessing in the heavenly places'. 'In Christ' he chose us, adopted us, redeemed us, made known to us the mystery of his will, and has given us a predestined inheritance. Christ cannot be separated from his blessings.

No one has better understood this than John Calvin. In a memorable passage in his *Institutes*, Calvin writes almost lyrically about the 'whole salvation' that God has provided for this fallen, lost world in his Son Jesus Christ. Read these following words slowly and prayerfully:

> We see that our whole salvation and all its parts are comprehended in Christ (Acts 4:12). We should therefore take care not to derive the least portion of it from anywhere else. If we seek salvation, we are taught by the very name of Jesus that it is 'of him' (1 Cor. 1:30). If we seek any other gifts of the Spirit, they will be found in his anointing. If we seek strength, it lies in his dominion; if purity, in his conception; if gentleness, it appears in his birth. For by his birth he was made like us in all respects (Heb. 2:17) that he might learn to feel our pain (Heb. 5:2). If we seek redemption, it lies in his passion; if acquittal, in his condemnation; if remission of the curse, in his cross (Gal. 3:13); if satisfaction, in his sacrifice; if purification, in his blood; if reconciliation, in his descent into hell; if mortification of the flesh, in his tomb; if newness of life, in his resurrection; if immortality, in the same; if inheritance of the heavenly kingdom, in his entrance into heaven; if protection, if security, if abundant supply of all blessings, in his kingdom; if untroubled expectation of judgment, in the power given him to judge. In short, since rich store of every kind of good abounds in him, let

us drink our fill from this fountain, and from no other (II.xvi.19).

IAN HAMILTON
Inverness, April 2017

1. *God Is Trinity:*
The Gospel's God

One of the remarkable features of the early church was its preoccupation with the doctrine of God. Initially the concern of men like Athanasius (AD 300–371) was to establish and defend the deity of Christ against men like Arius who taught that Jesus was a creature. Athanasius believed that Arius did not understand the Scriptures. He also understood that if Jesus was not God in the fullest sense, we have no Saviour and we are still in our sins. So at the Council of Nicea in 325 the church publicly acknowledged the teaching of God's word that Jesus was 'homoousios', of the same substance or being as the Father, that is, equally God (read John 1:1-2).

This, however, was only the beginning of the church's exploration of the Bible's teaching about God. During the remainder of the fourth century and well into the fifth, the church came increasingly to acknowledge both the unity and plurality of God's self-revelation. The climax of these explorations came in the statements of the Council of Chalcedon in 451. In these statements, the biblical doctrine of the Holy Trinity was profoundly and beautifully explained. God is truly one, but he is also truly three. He is not three gods but one God in three persons, Father, Son and Holy Spirit.

This foundational biblical truth absolutely separates Christianity from Islam. In Islam, Allah is a solitary being, a monad. Because he is a monad he cannot be love, for who was there for him to love in eternity? But 'God is love' (1 John 4:8). In eternity the Father loved the Son and the Son loved the Father. The Son loved the Spirit and the Spirit loved the Son. The Father loved the Spirit and the Spirit loved the Father. God is a communion of love, an eternal, outgoing communion of love.

From Genesis 1, where God's unity and plurality are adumbrated, to John 1:1-18, where the mystery of God's plurality in unity is most revealed, God declares himself to be a communion of three persons, equal in glory, majesty and power, and equally worthy of praise, honour, worship, and service.

So far, so good. But what does the doctrine of the Holy Trinity have to do with my everyday life? Throughout the centuries some professing Christians have thought and taught that the truth of God's triunity is at best a theological speculation and at worst an irrelevance to daily life. Nothing could be further from the truth. There is no truth more vital to a Christian's life, no truth more calculated to enrich, deepen, and delight a Christian's heart than the doctrine of the Holy Trinity. Believers and their children are baptised into the *one* name of the Father, the Son and the Holy Spirit (Matt. 28:18-20). Christians are chosen, saved, and sealed by the triune God (Eph. 1:3-14; Heb. 9:14). Christian worship is directed to the Father, through the Son, and in the grace and power of the Spirit (Eph. 2:18).

Much could be said, but note this one thing: our Lord Jesus Christ taught that eternal life is to know God (John 17:3). But God is triune; he is not a monad. Jesus is teaching us that eternal life is not endless existence but life in fellowship with the triune God. Knowing God as Father, Son and Holy Spirit is eternal life. What could possibly be more exhilarating than that?

If you knew, personally and intimately, the Queen of England, you would be deeply honoured and the envy of many. If you had access freely into her presence, you would be, in the truest sense of the word, a 'celebrity'. A Christian has intimate fellowship with the triune God. A Christian has freedom of access, night and day, into the presence of the one who made the uncountable myriad of stars. A Christian possesses the unending, unfailing love of the triune God, a love that will never end because it never began (Jer. 31:3). And the astonishing thing about this love is that it is the very love with which the Father loves his Son (John 17:23, 26).

The Christian life is a life of communion with the Father who loved and loves us, with the Son who gave himself for us and who ever lives to protect and bless us, and with the Holy Spirit who brings us into the communion of the Holy Trinity and makes it his special delight to glorify Christ in us and to us (John 16:14).

Is there anything in life to rival such astounding privilege? John Owen wrote, 'Our greatest hindrance in the Christian life is not our lack of effort, but our lack of acquaintedness with our privileges.' How right he was! Your and my greatest privilege in life, this life and the life to come, is to know the Holy Trinity and, even more wonderfully, to be known by the Holy Trinity. May the triune God, Father, Son and Holy Spirit, give us all the grace to become more personally acquainted with our privileges, the greatest of which is knowing this triune God to be our God.

2. What Is a Christian?
Gospel Foundations

As we embark on our gospel-shaped journey, we need to be clear, absolutely clear, about one thing. The question, 'What is a Christian?' has been given many answers, most of them having little to do with what the Bible says a Christian is. The Bible, it is true, has several ways to describe a Christian. A Christian is a forgiven sinner, a new creation in Christ, an adopted child of God, a heaven-bound pilgrim, and much more besides.

One of the most dramatic descriptions of a Christian, however, is found in Romans 6:13, where Paul tells us that a Christian, every Christian, is someone who has been 'brought from death to life'. Paul is making a categorical statement. He is not highlighting a possibility but declaring a fact, an accomplished, once for all, unrepeatable and undeniable fact. If you are a Christian, you have been 'brought from death to life'. You may not feel you have, but if you are a Christian you have!

First, what is this 'death' that Christians no longer live in? In the Bible death is principally a spiritual state. God said to Adam in the garden of Eden, 'of the tree of the knowledge of good and evil you shall not eat, for in the day that you eat of it *you shall surely die*' (Gen. 2:17). Adam ate the forbidden fruit (God was testing Adam's obedience), and he died. Physically, the process of death began to take over his life, but spiritually, at that moment he died. Death is the state of alienation from God. Death is the lifestyle of separation from God, the lifestyle of rebellion against the sovereign lordship of God. More than this, however, death is a dominion, a kingdom ruled over by a king, Satan. This is the kingdom that every single one of us belonged to because of our union with Adam our first head. When he disobeyed God, we disobeyed God in him. He was the head of humanity and when he fell, we all fell; 'in Adam all die' (1 Cor. 15:22).

Second, what is this 'life' that Christians have been brought into? Just as life is the opposite of death, so this 'life' which Christians have been brought into is the opposite of alienation from God and rebellion against his lordship. 'Life' is the sphere where separation from God is replaced by fellowship with God, where alienation from God is replaced by friendship with God.

Third, this leads us to ask: how are we taken from death to life? Notice the phrase: 'have been brought from death to life'. The verb is in the passive mood, that is, we did not bring this transformation about; God did. By his gracious sovereign action God brought us out of death and into life. When did he do this? He did it effectively on Calvary's cross when God's Son paid the ransom price of our sin (Mark 10:45). In Adam we all died, but in Christ, our better Head, we were all raised to life (Rom. 6). In Christ, God accomplished our rescue from the kingdom of death and darkness (Col. 1:13). But we do not come into the possession of this rescue experientially until we believe on the Lord Jesus Christ and embrace him as Saviour and Lord (John 3:36; 1 John 5:1; Acts 16:30-31).

Two questions: Have you believed on the Lord Jesus Christ? Have you come to see and feel your need before God of his forgiveness and new life? Have you received the great salvation God holds out to everyone, everywhere, in his Son Jesus Christ?

Second, if you have, are you living as someone who has been brought from death into life? Would anyone looking at your life conclude that you had experienced a resurrection? The idea of resurrection is dramatic. Imagine meeting someone who had died but then been raised to life. The encounter would be dramatic, to say the least.

Every Christian is a resurrected man/woman. We have become partakers of the life of the risen Christ. The life of the world to come has already come and invaded our lives. What will such a life look like? Read Galatians 5:22-23 and Colossians 3:12-17. These two passages are remarkable and humbling word pictures of the Christian life. This is not something we will become in ten, twenty, thirty or in however so many years' time. This is how Christians are to live from the moment they are saved. Yes, we will fail, and at times fail badly. But if Jesus Christ dwells in us by his Spirit, his life is to shape and define your life and mine.

Now, stop what you are doing. Reflect. Meditate. Repent. Rejoice. By the grace and power of the Holy Spirit, be what you are: someone who has been raised from death to life.

3. A New Covenant Command: Gospel Fear

'Honour everyone. Love the brotherhood. Fear God. Honour the emperor' (1 Pet. 2:17). Most reading this will have some idea what it means to honour everyone, to love the brotherhood, and to honour the emperor. But how many know what it means to 'Fear God'? This is not an abstract or arcane question. We need to know what it is to fear God for at least two reasons: First, 'the fear of the LORD is the beginning of knowledge' (Prov. 1:7). Second, 'the LORD takes pleasure in those who fear him' (Psa. 147:11). If you don't know, in some true measure, what it is to fear God your knowledge, above all of God, is impoverished and God will not take pleasure in you.

It has not been common in the past forty or so years to read books or to hear sermons devoted to the subject of the fear of God, not least within evangelical Christianity. This is both sad and surprising. It is surprising because the New Testament tells us that holiness is brought to completion in 'the fear of God' (2 Cor. 7:1) and every Christian is called to be holy as God himself is holy (1 Pet. 1:15; Heb. 12:14). It is sad because the absence of the fear of God in the life of the church has led to a vast impoverishment in the quality of the church's worship and in the moral character of professing evangelicals. If one of the hallmarks of new covenant worship is that we worship God 'with reverence and awe' (Heb. 12:28-29), we greatly need to see the fear of God recovered in the life, worship, witness, and service of the church.

Throughout the Bible, believers are identified again and again as those who fear God. One of the promises of the new covenant was that God would put the fear of him in the hearts of his people 'that they may not turn from me' (Jer. 32:40).

I hardly need to say that this fear of God has nothing to do with a cringing, fearful, uncertain attitude to God. God is our Father in Christ. He loves his people with an everlasting love (Jer. 31:3). He rejoices over his people with loud singing (Zeph. 3:17). He spared not his only Son but gave him up for us all (Rom. 8:32). The last thing God wants is for his blood-redeemed children to cringe in fearful uncertainty before him.

Nor does the fear of God mean joyless, dull, even lugubrious worship. Christian worship should always be vibrant, joyful, heart-expanding and mind-enlarging. How can it not be when we are worshipping God, the all-glorious Holy Trinity, 'majestic in holiness, awesome in glorious deeds, doing wonders' (Exod. 15:11)?

What then does it mean to fear God? Very simply, to fear God is to honour him as God and to worship him 'with reverence and awe' (Heb. 12:28). What that means in daily living is to love what he loves and to hate what he hates and to prize his 'Well done' above all the accolades of this world, making his glory the chief business of one's life.

This truth is worked out on the horizontal as well as on the vertical plane. In Nehemiah 5:15 we read, 'The former governors who were before me laid heavy burdens on the people and took from them for their daily ration forty shekels of silver. Even their servants lorded it over the people. But I did not do so, *because of the fear of God.*' Because Nehemiah feared God he refused to use his privileged position for personal gain. He treated those under him with generosity and dignity (read the whole passage). Men and women are God's image-bearers and are to be treated as such. Fearing the Lord, treating him with due reverence and awe, will inevitably (and I do mean *inevitably*) deeply influence the way we live among our fellow image-bearers.

The Bible is full of examples and illustrations of men and women who feared God. Abraham feared God when he obeyed God's command to leave his family, friends, and culture and go to a land he knew nothing about. Moses feared God when he obeyed God's command to go to Egypt and said to the most powerful man on earth, 'God says, "Let my people go."' Gideon feared God when at God's command he confronted a huge army with only 300 men. David feared God when he challenged Goliath who was defying the living God. Daniel, Hannaniah, Mishael, and Azariah feared God when they refused to conform to the pagan practices in Babylon, even though their refusal could have led to their death. Jeremiah feared God when he confronted God's people and their spiritual shepherds with their godless hypocrisy at the risk of his own life. Paul feared God when he stood before Felix and 'reasoned about righteousness and self-control and the coming judgment' (Acts 24:25). Above all, our Lord Jesus Christ feared God by being 'obedient to the point of death, even death on a cross' (Phil. 2:8). He above all others perfectly epitomised what it meant to fear God—he chose the will of his Father, lovingly, even though that obedience would cost him everything.

At the heart of the fear of God there is a driving, compelling pulse beat. What makes men and women fear God is not, first, that he has absolute rights over their life, though he has. They fear God, above all, because he loves them and they love him. That God should love us is a wonder of all wonders. He is the thrice-holy One. He is of purer eyes than to look on sin. And yet he 'so loved the world that he gave his only Son'. It is little wonder John wrote, 'In this is love, not that we have loved God but that he loved us and sent his Son to be the propitiation for our sins' (1 John 4:10). It is when God's love is poured out into our hearts through the Holy Spirit (Rom. 5:5) that we begin truly to fear God, to hold him in reverence and awe (Heb. 12:28).

The fear of God and love to God are inextricably joined. Love to God that does not honour him as God and does not live in happy obedience to his royal commandments, is not truly love to God (John 14:15). The fear of God that is not suffused with heart love to God is not the fear of God that the Bible tells us is a mark of a true believer.

Properly speaking, the fear of God is the *fruit* of the gospel. It is only when we come, or better, are brought, to receive the Lord Jesus Christ as Saviour and Lord that we begin to give to God the reverence and awe that is his due.

How else would a forgiven sinner, an adopted child of God, respond to the God of saving, justifying, sanctifying grace?

'Fear God'! He is worthy of your fear, your loving, thankful, worshipful, reverent obedience.

> Fear Him, ye saints, and you will then
>   Have nothing else to fear;
> Make you His service your delight,
>   Your wants shall be His care.

4. Isaiah's Life-Changing Encounter: The Gospel's Transforming Power

No two Christians have an identical spiritual pathology. There is nothing formulaic about the way God brings sinners into a saving relationship with himself. That said, every Christian will, to a greater or lesser degree, identify with Isaiah's dramatic encounter with God, recorded for us in Isaiah 6:1-13. Like Saul of Tarsus' conversion, recorded in Acts 9, the significance of Isaiah's encounter with the living God (see John 12:41) did not lie in its drama but in its decisiveness.

The date of Isaiah 6 is the middle years of the eighth century BC. King Uzziah has died. But the most significant event in that year was not the king's death but Isaiah's call to the prophetic ministry. King Uzziah had died, but the only King who really mattered continued to reign and to bring his living word to people who 'walked in darkness' (Isa. 9:2).

There are a number of features in these verses with which every Christian can surely identify.

First, Isaiah came face to face with the exalted majesty of God (John 12:41). This is where the Christian life first takes root. Every Christian is a man or woman mastered by the exalted greatness and majesty of God ('*Deus subegit*', 'God subdued me', to use John Calvin's evocative phrase). This is true especially of men set apart to be preachers and teachers in God's church. Ministers of Christ, as all servants of Christ, are men humbled by the knowledge of God's exalted majesty (Exod. 15:11). It is out of a Spirit-wrought sense of God's exalted greatness that Christian living and all Christian ministry is to flow.

Second, Isaiah was personally overwhelmed by his encounter with the exalted majesty of God: 'Woe is me! For I am lost' (verse 5). The majesty of God was not simply a doctrine Isaiah acknowledged, it was a power, a glory, he had experienced. It is in this soil that Christian usefulness in general flourishes. This is certainly true for the pastoral ministry. Preaching is essentially the overflow of a man's life. No amount of intellectual ability or spiritual giftedness can substitute for a life that has been overwhelmed by a personal sense of God's glory, resulting in a personal, and deepening, sense of the sinfulness of sin.

Third, Isaiah experienced the forgiving, renewing and equipping grace of God. Spiritual gifts will only be blessed by God when they are exercised under his sovereign majesty and out of a life humbled by a deep sense of unfitness. When Paul called himself 'the chief of sinners' (1 Tim. 1:15 KJV), he did not say, 'I *was*' but 'I *am*'! He was not being falsely humble; he was speaking as a man who had come face to face with his own sinfulness and had discovered the amazing grace of God in Christ.

This, I think, is the first prerequisite for exercising a preaching ministry. Christian ministers are to speak as men who have experienced the wonder of God's forgiving grace in Christ. It is this perhaps more than anything else that knocks the conceit out of us. In 1 Corinthians 3:5, Paul writes, 'What then is Apollos? What is Paul?' Not '*who*' are Apollos and Paul, but '*what*' are they? He answers, 'Servants [*only* servants!] through whom you believed.' This is the testimony of a man who has come face to face with God, been humbled to the dust, and then discovered the restoring, renewing grace of God.

Fourth, Isaiah offered himself unreservedly to the ministry of God's word. 'Unconditionalism' is a fundamental element in Christian living: 'Here am I! Send me' (Isa. 6:8; Matt. 10:37-39). The church was worth Christ's blood; it is worth our unconditional labours. There is an inevitable cost to faithful Christian living and serving in a fallen world. Jesus never wearied of telling his disciples that the cost of belonging to him and serving him would be great (John 15:18-21). The cost, potential and real, will only ever be embraced when the glory of God's being and the sheer grace of his forgiving, renewing mercy in Christ overwhelm us. Have they overwhelmed you?

Fifth, Isaiah was given a daunting commission (verses 9-13). He was sent to bring God's word of judgment to a spiritually-corrupt and morally-debased church and world. It was a message of solemn judgment. However, the last word would not be judgment but mercy (verse 13b).

The gospel is double-edged (John 3:36). Judgment and mercy stand together at the heart of the gospel: God's awful judgment on sin in his Son, and his awesome mercy also in his Son. But it must never be forgotten that 'God did not send his Son into the world to condemn the world' (John 3:17). The great note at the heart of every authentic Christian life and service is mercy. God is rich in mercy (Eph. 2:4).

Tradition says that Isaiah was eventually 'sawn in two'. For him the cost of faithful service was great. But how else could a man live who had seen 'the Lord sitting upon a throne, high and lifted up', and who had received unimaginable mercy? The cost may well be great, but the reward is beyond price: 'Well done, good and faithful servant … Enter into the joy of your master' (Matt. 25:21).

5. The Duplex Gratia:
The Gospel's Double Grace

One of the most remarkable statements in the Bible is Ephesians 1:3. There we are told that 'in Christ', God has blessed his people with 'every spiritual blessing in the heavenly places'. '*Every* spiritual blessing', nothing lacking, is the present possession of everyone who is savingly united to Jesus Christ. There is no truth more basic and more profound in the gospel.

No one has better expressed the significance of this than John Calvin. Calvin taught that by his death and resurrection Christ procured for his people a 'double grace' (*duplex gratia*). His fundamental statement on this matter is found in his *Institutes*:

> Christ was given to us by God's generosity, to be grasped and possessed by us in faith. By partaking of him, we principally receive a double grace: namely, that being reconciled to God through Christ's blamelessness, we may have in heaven instead of a Judge a gracious Father; and secondly, that sanctified by Christ's spirit we may cultivate blamelessness and purity of life.[1]

It is absolutely true that justification and sanctification are always to be distinguished. However, they must never

[1] John Calvin, *Institutes of the Christian Religion* III.xi.1.

be separated. They belong together, having been given together, in the one, multi-complex, spiritual inheritance all believers receive through their union with Christ. From this foundational perspective, sanctification, what Calvin often refers to as 'regeneration', is not so much the fruit of justification as its constant companion, its inseparable twin.

Calvin makes plain that both justification (being 'reconciled to God through Christ's blamelessness') and sanctification (the cultivation 'of blamelessness and purity of life') are two aspects of the one gift of Christ. The spiritual simultaneity in Christ of the *duplex gratia* is strikingly highlighted later in the *Institutes*:

> These benefits are joined together by an everlasting and indissoluble bond, so that those whom he illumines by his wisdom he redeems; those whom he redeems, he justifies; those whom he justifies, he sanctifies. ... Although we may distinguish them, Christ contains both of them inseparably in himself. Do you wish, then, to attain righteousness in Christ? You must first possess Christ; but you cannot possess him without being made partaker of his sanctification, because he cannot be divided into pieces.[1]

Calvin makes the same point in his Commentary on 1 Corinthians:

---

[1] *Institutes* III.xvi.1, quoting 1 Cor. 1:13.

> For these fruits of grace are connected together, as it were, by an indissoluble tie, so that he who attempts to sever them does in a manner tear Christ in pieces. Let therefore the man who seeks to be justified through Christ, by God's unmerited goodness, consider that this cannot be attained without his taking him at the same time for sanctification.[1]

The importance of this *duplex gratia* for Calvin is not merely one of exegetical and doctrinal exactness. He understands that because we receive Christ for justification and sanctification simultaneously, this truth is enough to refute those who slanderously claimed that he and the other Reformers taught a 'free justification' that 'called men off from good works'.[2]

If this basic, foundational biblical truth had been grasped by evangelical Christians, it would be immediately obvious that any professed justification by grace through faith that did not manifest itself in true godliness is a complete sham. The great need is not to introduce talk about 'a future justification based on works', but rightly to teach what it means to be united to Christ and to receive in that faith-union 'every spiritual blessing'.

According to Calvin, justification is only logically prior to sanctification. It makes sanctification possible, and also makes it necessary. Between the two there is a significant difference. Justification is incapable of growth; it is an

[1] See *Comm.* on 1 Cor. 1:30.
[2] *Ibid.*

unrepeatable declaration that we are just before God in Christ. Sanctification is capable of growth; every Christian is to grow in the grace and knowledge of the Lord Jesus Christ (2 Pet. 3:18). There is no time, however, when a person is justified and not being sanctified. No time when a person is being sanctified and not already justified.

Justification does not cause sanctification. Sanctification does not commence after justification but simultaneously with justification. Each is given directly by Christ. Yet, they are inseparable gifts, two gifts wrapped together. In fact, one gift with two inseparable dimensions.

The *duplex gratia* signals the essential richness of the gospel and, more significantly, the fact that 'in Christ' believers receive everything that God has to give. He has nothing to give us outside of his Son, who is himself the gospel in all its fullness.

Far from leaving us in a state of static inertia, the *duplex gratia* summons us to sink our hearts and minds into the vast riches that we possess in our union with Christ, whom God made our wisdom and our righteousness and sanctification and redemption (1 Cor. 1:30). So Calvin writes,

> Let then the faithful learn to embrace him, not only for justification, but also for sanctification, as he has been given to us for both these purposes, lest they should render him asunder by their mutilated faith.[1]

---

[1] *Comm.* on Rom. 8:13.

It is little wonder that Paul is constrained to write: 'Blessed be the God and Father of our Lord Jesus Christ, who has blessed us in Christ with every spiritual blessing' (Eph. 1:3). Blessing God (literally 'eulogising' God) is the heartfelt expression of every life captured and captivated by the *duplex gratia*. But more importantly, this double grace reminds us to look for no grace outside of the Lord Jesus Christ. He is our all in all.

6. The God Who Hides Himself: Trusting the God of the Gospel

If any one phrase sums up the substance of the Bible it is, 'Behold your God'. In the Bible, the living God, the Creator of all that is, the Holy One who inhabits eternity, makes himself known. He has done this that we all might know him, come to love him, and find in him our greatest good. He has no need of us; we don't make him complete or fill up some lack in him. But he has revealed himself that we might know and love him here and now, and when we die enter into his nearer presence to 'enjoy him for ever'.

But God's revelation of himself is disturbing as well as wonderfully encouraging. It is encouraging beyond words when he tells us that he is 'merciful and gracious, slow to anger, and abounding in steadfast love and faithfulness' (Exod. 34:6). But it is disturbing when he tells us that he is a God who hides himself (Isa. 45:15). Blaise Pascal wrote: 'A religion which does not affirm that God is hidden is not true ... and a religion which does not offer the reason [for this hiddenness] is not illuminating.'[1] Pascal knew his Bible!

These sobering words, 'Truly, you are a God who hides himself', occur in a striking context. Isaiah is looking forward to a time when God's people, Israel, will be carried off into exile (Isa. 40–66 is, in the main, prophecy). For centuries Israel had provoked the Lord with their disobedience and shallow, superficial religion (1:10-20). They had, time after time, gone after other gods, imitated the godless world around them, and honoured God with their lips while their hearts were far from him (29:13). But remarkably the Lord refused to abandon them utterly. Even when he sent them into exile in Babylon, he continued to send them faithful prophets who courageously called them to repentance. More than that, the Lord held out to them a future rich in unimaginable hope and promise (45:14).

This is the context to Isaiah's words in 45:15. As God's prophet looked at the world around him, as he contemplated the prospect of God's people being sent into exile, as he pondered the promise that one day the mighty enemies of God's people 'shall come over to you and be

---

[1] *Pensées*, 586.

yours' (45:14), he is constrained to say, 'Truly, you are a God who hides himself.'

There is much for us to learn and take to heart from this particular revelation of God.

First, in 'hiding' himself, God is being who he is. God in himself is beyond our fathoming. 'Who has known the mind of the Lord?' (Rom. 11:34). God is incomprehensible. We can know him *truly* but never *exhaustively*. God is God! He hides himself not because he is contrary, or obtuse, or deliberately mysterious. He is essentially beyond our understanding and enquiring. Behold your God!

Second, God does not act according to the canons of our understanding (Isa. 55:8-9). He always acts according to his own wisdom. He does what he does, not because he consults us or is trying to impress us, but because he alone knows what is best for his people. Jesus is the wisdom of God (1 Cor. 1:30-31). But who saw God's saving, cosmic wisdom when they looked at the cross?

Third, God acts within the flow of human history. What I mean is that behind all the twists and turns of history and the convulsions of nations, God is carrying out his 'grand design'. Because we are who we are, sinful creatures, our understanding is always flawed to a degree. Even as forgiven sinners we see through a glass darkly. Our knowledge is limited and lacking. We are like little children watching a master craftsman create a beautiful piece of furniture; the first strokes of the chisel seem terribly destructive, when in fact they are necessary to secure the finished article. As we look out on our chaotic world with all its mayhem and tragedy, our great need is to know and to be persuaded that our God is perfectly wise and wisely perfect in all he does. 'As for God, his way is perfect' (Psa. 18:30 KJV). This is where 'faith' comes in. Faith in the absolute trustworthiness of the Bible is not a vacuous thing. Faith understands that because the Bible is the word of God, it can always be trusted to speak truth to us.

Fourth, God acts ultimately to secure the eternal good of his saved people (Isa. 45:16-17). In pursuing his ultimate purpose to bless his people, God has many decreed objectives, one of which is to train us to live by faith and not by sight. This necessarily means that he places the template of his Son's believing and faithful life over ours. Why do I say 'necessarily'? God's purpose for each one of us is to conform us to the image of his Son (Rom. 8:29). This will mean that the trustful obedience that marked our Saviour's life even as his own Father hid himself as he hung on the cross, is to be etched into our lives. Jesus' cry of abandonment was the height of his trustful, believing obedience. He never murmured, complained, or expressed any resentment. He was bewildered, but never once did he either demur or disobey. He was always the trusting obedient Servant Son. In all of God's dealings with you and with me, he is pursuing his purpose to make us like his Son.

When he hides himself, the Lord is not being capricious or callous. He is always our loving, ever kind and merciful heavenly Father. God isn't hidden because we are too stupid to find him, or too lazy, or not 'spiritual' enough. He hides himself for his own reasons, and he reveals himself for his own perfectly wise and good reasons too. If that were not so, God would not be God; God would be nothing more than a projection of our own religious ideas and wishes. This is why Paul's doxology in Romans 11:33-36 should be etched on the hearts and minds of all Christians. God is God and he is, in Christ, our good and always gracious God. So when he is pleased to hide himself, let us walk by faith and not by sight (2 Cor. 5:7).

7. Loved with Everlasting Love: The Gospel's Wonder

Some years ago I was sitting in a ministers' conference enjoying very much hearing God's word preached with grace and power. The preacher, a dear friend, paused and said something that riveted me. He quoted some words of Geerhardus Vos: 'The reason God will never stop loving you is that he never began.' Vos was reflecting on Jeremiah 31:3: 'I have loved you with an everlasting love.' I suppose I had read those words many times and in prayer had blessed the Lord for loving me with an everlasting love. But the truth Vos drew out from those words all but overwhelmed me.

It is a biblical commonplace that God is love. It is a gospel commonplace that 'God so loved the world that he gave his only Son.' But how much of a commonplace in our lives is the fact and knowledge and joy of God's love? If God's love for his people in Christ (he has never loved us outside of Christ) truly is an everlasting love, a love that has no beginning and will have no end, do we sufficiently allow that astonishing truth to impact our minds, amaze our hearts, and transform our lives?

Perhaps more than anything else this truth is intended to breathe unfailing assurance and hope into our often distempered lives. Life for a Christian in a fallen world can be difficult. There are times when remaining sin seems to rule over us, though its rule has been decisively broken in our union with Christ in his death and resurrection. There are times when our circumstances seem all against us, when it is a victory simply to get through the day. There are times when dark disappointments threaten to overwhelm us and leave us angry with God, protesting that if he really cared he would not have withheld some hoped-for blessing from our lives. At such times we need to stop and recall to our minds Jeremiah 31:3, 'I have loved you with an everlasting love.'

God's love for his believing children, all of them, is the bedrock of sane and assured godly living. It is an anchor that keeps us firmly attached to our God. Not an anchor that will keep you from being buffeted by life's violent storms; but an anchor that will keep you from being wrecked by those storms. In the midst of life's unexpected trials and troubles, our greatest need is not an explanation of why, but an assurance that, come what may, nothing will separate us from God's love in Christ Jesus (Rom. 8:38-39).

One of Satan's most destructive ploys is to sow seeds of doubt in our minds that God really and truly loves us. Most often he uses disappointments and the world's relentless hostility to suggest that God has abandoned us, or at best has lost interest in us: 'Would a God who really cared allow this situation, this person, to afflict you?' At such times we need to redirect our minds to the truth of God's everlasting love and bathe our souls in its refreshing truth. Above all we need to take ourselves to where that everlasting love most manifests itself, in the cross of our Lord Jesus. The cross was not the place where Jesus won for us the heavenly Father's love. The cross was where the heavenly Father's love was displayed in all its unfathomable magnificence. It was because *God so loved* the world *that he gave* his only Son!

It is the most wonderful of things to know that you are loved unconditionally and eternally. Not unconditionally in the sense that no matter how we live God will still love us. If we live any way we choose, we simply show that our great need is to be born again and saved from the coming wrath. But our heavenly Father does love even his errant children—and in that love will chastise us 'that we may share his holiness' (Heb. 12:10).

It is little wonder that John writes: '[Behold] what kind of love the Father has given to us, that we should be called children of God; and so we are' (1 John 3:1). Wonder of wonders!

8. *Extravagant Grace:*
The Scandal of the Gospel

It is a salutary experience to read the books of Kings and Chronicles. King after king after king lived in almost unbroken defiance of, and rebellion against, the Lord. He had chosen Israel, entered into covenant with the nation, given the people his law, provided for them the sin-atoning sacrifices, and settled them in a land flowing with milk and honey. What did the nation and especially its leaders do in return? Read Kings and Chronicles and be stunned into silence at the unimaginable wickedness that covered the face of the land. The wickedness reached a climactic moment in the reign of Manasseh, the son of Hezekiah. In 2 Kings 21 you can read about the life of godless vileness that Manasseh pursued with relish. Read this chapter and marvel that God did not wipe him and the nation from the face of the earth.

Now read 2 Chronicles 33 and be even more stunned. The Chronicler tells us what the writer of Kings does not—Manasseh, wicked, vile, godless, child-sacrificing Manasseh, repented, turned to the Lord, and found mercy.

This is what happened. On account of his unbounded wickedness, the Lord had Manasseh bound, tied by hooks, and led into captivity in Babylon. 'And when he was in distress, he entreated the favour of the LORD his God and humbled himself greatly before the God of his fathers. He prayed to him; and God was moved by his entreaty and heard his plea and brought him again to Jerusalem into his kingdom. Then Manasseh knew that the LORD was God' (2 Chron. 33:12-13). If it wasn't in the Bible, God's own living and true word, you would never believe it.

The grace of God is unimaginably glorious and scandalous. Manasseh! If ever there was a man 'plucked from the fire', rescued from the suburbs of hell, it was Manasseh. It is the conversion of a man like Manasseh that searches out our understanding of God's grace. Do we really believe that

> The vilest offender who truly believes,
> That moment from Jesus a pardon receives?

God's grace is deeply unsettling as well as wonderfully reassuring. We read about Manasseh, and before him King David (an adulterous murderer), both of whom found grace in the eyes of God. Their experience of God's astonishing grace poses a pastoral question to the church: How ready are we to 'receive sinners'? We say we are, but how ready and willing are we? Do we, like our Lord, hold out our hands all the day long to a lost, God-denying, vile and wicked world? We say we do, but does the lost world around us see that we do? One of the Pharisees' great complaints about Jesus was, 'This man receives sinners' (Luke 15:2)—and he certainly did.

It is one thing to have a theology of grace and another to live grace. There is, of course, a danger in preaching grace and living grace. Too often the extravagance of God's grace has become an excuse for living a lawless life. Paul was probably responding to this heresy when he wrote, 'Are we to continue in sin that grace may abound? By no means!' (Rom. 6:1-2). But it is quite impossible to continue in sin if you have been the recipient of God's extravagant grace, because 'How can we who died to sin still live in it?' (Rom. 6:2). In salvation, the God of grace unites us to the Lord Jesus Christ, the Saviour who died to sin (Rom. 6:10). If you are living lightly or heedlessly of God's law, it is a sure sign that you have as yet never known the saving grace of God, the grace that plants within us what Thomas Chalmers referred to as 'the expulsive power of a new affection'.

The question we must all ask ourselves is, How would my church, how would I, cope with an influx of world-stained sinners? We like things in the church to be just as we think they should be, that is, just what makes us comfortable. Of course, God's word must alone shape the life, worship, and ministry of the church. But how adaptable are we? How ready and willing are we to start where people are and not where we would like them to be?

God's grace is unsettling. The apostles were at first reluctant to think that Saul of Tarsus, who trampled the church like a wild boar and was implicated in Stephen's martyrdom, could possibly be converted. But God had saved him and made him a new man in Christ.

For many of us the problem is not in confessing the extravagance of God's grace, but in practising and embracing that grace in our relationships with 'sinners'. God's grace in Christ is deeply unsettling.

The life of Manasseh has much to teach us. Read 2 Kings 21 and 2 Chronicles 33. Read, reflect, and pray that you will not only *preach* the grace of God but *live* the grace of God.

9. *Trust and Obey: Gospel Inseparables*

From beginning to end the Christian life is a life of faith. 'We walk by faith, not by sight', Paul wrote to the church in Corinth (2 Cor. 5:7). But what did he mean? What does it mean to walk by faith and not by sight? To walk by faith is to live your life on the basis of the faithful character of God and the absolute trustworthiness of his promises. This is what it means to live as a Christian, refusing to believe what your eyes tell you when what you see appears to oppose what God has promised, and challenges the essential goodness of his character.

This life-principle is perhaps nowhere more graphically and dramatically illustrated than in the life of Abraham. God commanded Abraham to take his son, his only son, Isaac, whom he loved, and offer him as a burnt offering (Gen. 22). Apart from God's command seeming to conflict with his character, Isaac was not only Abraham's only son, he was the son in whom God's promise to bless all the nations was established (Gen. 12:2-3). What was Abraham to do? He believed God: 'No distrust made him waver concerning the promise of God, but he grew strong in his faith as he gave glory to God, fully convinced that God was able to do what he had promised' (Rom. 4:20-21).

Christian faith always has a direct object: the absolute trustworthiness of God's character and the absolute inviolability of his promises. As Abraham faced this unnerving and soul-searching test, he grew strong in his faith as he gave glory to God. In other words, faith is nurtured and nourished as it ponders God's being and rejoices in his attributes. This is what it means to live by faith. The faithful Christian is the trusting Christian. The faithful Christian is the Christian who obeys God even when their circumstances seem to be all against them.

Too often we allow ourselves to be dispirited by the shallowness and variableness of our faith. I do not mean that our shallow and variable faith should not humble us. But too often we spend more time looking *in* to ourselves than looking *out* to our God and nourishing our faith in the glory of who God is and what he has done for us in our Lord Jesus Christ. The primary focus of faith, and what most strengthens faith, is faith's direct object—the unfailingly good and gracious God who spared not his only Son but gave him up for us all.

One of Satan's well-rehearsed strategies is to turn us in upon ourselves, to absorb us with our weaknesses and sinful failures. Too often we fall into this quagmire and find it hard to extricate ourselves. When the Lord convicts us of our sinful failures and failings, he immediately points us away from ourselves to himself. This is what nurtures and nourishes our faith—not dwelling on our sins, but dwelling on the one who freely and fully forgives our sins and who delights to embrace us in his unfailing love.

Are your circumstances shouting out to you that God doesn't care, that he has forgotten you? Do your circumstances seem to mock God's promises? Be like Abraham: give glory to God. As the old hymn so well puts it,

> Trust and obey,
> For there's no other way
> To be happy in Jesus,
> But to trust and obey.

Theologically, if not always grammatically, faith takes a direct object. And faith's direct object is the God who cannot lie, whose promises are all yes, and yes again, in Christ Jesus (cf. 2 Cor. 1:20). Live by faith and you will die a conqueror.

10. Resisting a Diet of False Illusions: The Need for Gospel Saturation

Why did John Calvin preach up to eight times a week in Geneva? Eight times a week? How did he make the time? Was he not writing commentaries on almost every book of the Bible? Was he not writing treatises on numerous theological and pastoral subjects? Was he not the Reformation's premier letter-writer, writing to hundreds of Christians, kings, queens, and nobles, as well as pastors and their families? Eight times a week!

Calvin did not think he was doing anything extraordinary in preaching eight (sometimes more) times a week. He was persuaded that if the church was to survive in a hostile world, bombarded on all sides by siren voices, saying, 'Don't be so serious, lighten up, return to Mother Church (Rome)', then God's people needed to be saturated in the word of God.

With other Reformers, Calvin believed that only being exposed to God's word once or twice a week did little to resist the relentless diet of false illusions emanating from the world. He was persuaded that Christians needed all the time they could give to hearing God's word.

I wonder if Calvin's thinking resonates with you. We live in a culture full to overflowing with false illusions. Most of the various forms of the modern media industry seek to deceive us (there are always honourable exceptions). Relentlessly the message goes out, dressed up so seductively, 'Without this, life is dull. Without this, you are missing out. With this, life will overflow with joy. Join this and you will never be the same man, woman, again.' And so the litany goes on. 'This is life', the music and style icons relentlessly tell us, and we are duped into thinking it might just be so.

In Romans 12:2, Paul exhorts us not to be conformed to this world, but to be transformed by the renewal of our minds. He is telling us that if our minds are not being renewed, then we will be squeezed into the mould of this fallen, passing world. Perhaps more than any previous generation of Christians, our generation needs to be saturated in the wisdom, grace, goodness, and health-giving clarity of God's truth. We need our minds decluttered and then refreshed by the 'wisdom that comes down from above' (James 3:15).

We live in a world of deceptive illusions—powerful, seductive illusions—that are out to ensnare us and kill us. Calvin was absolutely right: we need every given opportunity to hear God's living, clarifying, deception-scattering word.

So my question to you is this: Do you prize every given opportunity to hear God's word? You could read this as a rebuke, and in a measure you might be right in doing so. But, rather, see this question as a loving exhortation to hunt out every opportunity to sit under the ministry of God's word. Not because quantity matters more than quality; but because God himself speaks to us by his Spirit through his word every time it is faithfully proclaimed.

I have a good friend in the USA who was accused by some church members of being 'legalistic' because he encouraged them not to be satisfied with coming to worship once a week. His encouragement was not legalistic, it was the kind, thoughtful, caring encouragement of a pastor set apart to care for Christ's sheep. May we all be like the Psalmist who wrote, 'I was glad when they said to me, "Let us go to the house of the LORD!"' (Psa. 122:1).

11. 'This Is Our Beloved':
The Heart of the Gospel

Sometimes reading a Puritan author can take you into another world. The Puritans are not always the easiest of men to read, though the difficulty is often over-hyped. John Owen was possibly the greatest, and deepest, of the seventeenth-century pastor-theologians. In the second volume of his works, *Communion with God*,[1] Owen committed himself to doing what he believed no theologian had done before him. He sought to explicate from

---

[1] *The Works of John Owen, II: Communion with God* (1689; repr. London: Banner of Truth Trust, 1965).

Scripture the distinct communion that Christians have with the three persons of the Godhead. In the course of his rich and soul-expanding exposition, Owen, in a passage of lyrical beauty, seeks to explain the surpassing excellence of Jesus Christ with whom the believer has communion supremely in grace.[1]

Owen has been expounding the Christian's communion with Christ, showing from the Song of Songs how surpassingly excellent he is. Owen wants us to see and to feel the grace and loveliness of our Saviour. Take the time to read the lengthy piece and see if your heart and mind are not amazed at the escalating loveliness of the Lord Christ as Owen takes us on a tour of his excellencies.

Jesus Christ is, writes Owen:

> *Lovely in his person,*—in the glorious all-sufficiency of his Deity, gracious purity and holiness of his humanity, authority and majesty, love and power.
>
> *Lovely in his birth and incarnation*; when he was rich, for our sakes becoming poor,—taking part of flesh and blood, because we partook of the same; being made of a woman, that for us he might be made under the law, even for our sakes.
>
> *Lovely in the whole course of his life*, and the more than angelical holiness and obedience which, in the depth of poverty and persecution, he exercised therein;—doing good, receiving evil; blessing, and being cursed, reviled, reproached, all his days.

[1] Owen, *Works*, II.77-78.

Lovely in his death; yea, therein most lovely to sinners;—never more glorious and desirable than when he came broken, dead, from the cross. Then had he carried all our sins into a land of forgetfulness; then had he made peace and reconciliation for us; then had he procured life and immortality for us.

Lovely in his whole employment, in his great undertaking,—in his life, death, resurrection, ascension; being a mediator between God and us, to recover the glory of God's justice, and to save our souls,—to bring us to an enjoyment of God, who were set at such an infinite distance from him by sin.

Lovely in the glory and majesty wherewith he is crowned. Now he is set down at the right hand of the Majesty on high; where, though he be terrible to his enemies, yet he is full of mercy, love, and compassion, towards his beloved ones.

Lovely in all those supplies of grace and consolations, in all the dispensations of his Holy Spirit, whereof his saints are made partakers.

Lovely in all the tender care, power, and wisdom, which he exercises in the protection, safe-guarding, and delivery of his church and people, in the midst of all the oppositions and persecutions whereunto they are exposed.

Lovely in all his ordinances, and the whole of that spiritually glorious worship which he hath appointed to his people, whereby they draw nigh and have communion with him and his Father.

Lovely and glorious in the vengeance he taketh, and will finally execute, upon the stubborn enemies of himself and his people.

Lovely in the pardon he hath purchased and doth dispense,—in the reconciliation he hath established,—in the grace he communicates,—in the consolations he doth administer,—in the peace and joy he gives his saints,—in his assured preservation of them unto glory.

What shall I say? There is no end of his excellencies and desirableness;—'He is altogether lovely. This is our beloved, and this is our friend, O daughters of Jerusalem.'

This indeed is our Beloved.

12. Reasons Why You Should Not Believe: The Gospel and Unbelief

W hy would anyone in their right mind believe the Bible, believe Jesus Christ, and believe that belonging to a Christian church was a sane and sensible thing to do?

First reason why you shouldn't believe: The Bible is simply unbelievable. Who today in this modern, scientific, rational world believes in creation out of nothing by an eternal, omnipotent God? Who in their right mind believes that Adam and Eve lived in a special garden, sinned, and brought the whole creation crashing down with them? Are you serious? Who can possibly believe that God opened up a sea, led the Israelites through safely, but then drowned all their enemies in its waters? And then there is the story about the sun standing still: what is all that about? And Samson, killing hundreds of his enemies with the jawbone of a donkey! Could the Bible not have tried a little harder to make its message more believable?

Second reason why you shouldn't believe: Jesus Christ! God's Son from eternity. Born of a virgin. Feeder of 5,000-plus with a few loaves and fish. Healer of the sick. Raiser of the dead. He turned water into wine! He said he was the light of the world, the resurrection and the life, the way, the truth and the life. This is all just too fantastic to be true. It is claimed he rose from the dead and then (can you believe it?) ascended into heaven. He said he would 'come again' to judge the living and the dead. What is all that about? This is the modern world, not the Dark Ages! Jesus may have been a 'good man', but the Son of God, the Saviour of the world? Are you serious?

Third reason why you shouldn't believe: The Christian church! Look at it. At its best it is dull, boring, unexciting, an irrelevance to life in the modern world. People come together on a Sunday (some even do so twice!), sing, pray, and listen to someone 'explaining' the Bible for thirty to forty minutes. Get a life! What has that to offer anyone in today's world? Is it not just incredible that thinking people (so called) would do such a thing on a Sunday, when they could have a long lie-in, go to Starbucks, watch a movie, go out to the pub? And look at those Christians. They say they are the children of the living God, that he indwells their lives, that they are heading for God's eternal presence—would the way they live tell you that? If seeing is believing, then there is nothing to see in the church that would make anyone want to believe.

Reasons not to believe. And no doubt you can think of more. What can be said in defence of the Bible, Jesus Christ, and the church? Nothing. The Bible is a supernatural book. Jesus is a supernatural Saviour. The church is a supernatural people. They don't need defending, they simply are what they are. The Bible does not try to be relevant. Jesus did not try to appeal to the masses, or to anyone for that matter. The church with all its manifest weaknesses, of which there are many, is the people of God, his believing, blood-bought, saved, loved and loving people (and if this does not describe you, you are not truly a part of Christ's church).

Yes, there are reasons to believe, cogent, pressing, eminently reasonable reasons. But as Isaiah so plaintively declared, 'Who has believed what he has heard from us?' (Isa. 53:1). Unbelief is not a modern phenomenon. The world has never believed in the Bible or Jesus Christ or his church, until God in his mercy opens eyes to see, ears to hear and hearts to feel. Augustine was an unbelieving, pleasure-loving, sexually voracious philosopher until one day God in mercy broke into his life. He picked up the Bible, which he had read many times before, but this time what he read transformed his life. But you don't need to be an Augustine to believe in the Bible, Jesus Christ, and the Christian church. You do need to seek after the truth and to ask God, 'Be merciful to me, the sinner.' This for many is the ultimate stumbling-block. Pride not only swells a person's mind, it blinds them to the truth.

When I studied theology at the University of Edinburgh in the 1970s, one of my professors (and he was not the only one, sadly) wondered if it were possible in the modern world to believe in the Bible and in a supernatural Saviour, who died for the sins of his people and rose in triumph on the third day. I said I believed in those things, and there were many others like me. He thought I was 'out of my mind', but said so in a nice way. I thought he was a lost, poor, and to be pitied man who couldn't see past the limitations of his own mind.

The ultimate reason to believe in the Bible, Jesus Christ, and his church is simply this: they are everything they say they are. As the ancient Scots would say, 'Facts are chiels that winna ding ...'[1]

---

[1] A line from Robert Burns' poem 'A Dream': 'But facts are chiels that winna ding, An' downa be disputed' = 'But facts are fellows that will not be overturned, And cannot be disputed.'

13. When Is a Church Not a Church? Gospel Catholicity

Some years ago I attended the early morning Communion service in Magdalene College Chapel, Cambridge. The service was rich in trinitarian worship, in elevated God-centred prayers, in excellent hymns, and in a very fine, if all too brief sermon. As I sat and shared in the worship, this thought came to me: 'How diverse the church of Jesus Christ is!' Here was I, a head-to-toe Calvinist and a convinced Presbyterian, in a somewhat high Anglican College Chapel. The seeming incongruity set me thinking, and what follows is the substance of my thinking.

The *Westminster Confession of Faith* has a magnificent chapter (XXVI) entitled, 'Of the Communion of the Saints':

> All saints, that are united to Jesus Christ their Head, by His Spirit, and by faith, have fellowship with Him in His grace, sufferings, death, resurrection, and glory: and, being united to one another in love, they have communion in each other's gifts and graces, and are obliged to the performance of such duties, public and private, as do conduce to their mutual good, both in the inward and outward man. ... Which communion, as God offers

opportunity, is to be extended unto all those who, in every place, call upon the name of the Lord Jesus.

It is only too easy for Christians to exclude practically, and even principially, from the communion of the saints people in churches and denominations who do not believe what they believe. There are, of course, foundational and non-negotiable gospel doctrines. Paul writes in 1 Corinthians 15:1-3 of things that are 'of first importance'. There is a core of truths that belong to the essence of the Christian faith. If people deny any of these core truths they exclude themselves from the communion of the saints. But if they believe these truths and trust the Saviour imbedded in these truths, they are 'family' and must be acknowledged and embraced as such. They may have defective views of divine sovereignty, not understand the priority of grace over faith, have uncertain views of Genesis 1, have fantastical views on the end times and promote the continuation of charismatic gifts; but if they hold to Christ the head, they are family. If the Father has elected them, the Son has shed his blood for them, and they are indwelt by the Holy Spirit, they are family.

Family life can be problematic and, sadly, can be dysfunctional. But family *is* family no matter how problematic and dysfunctional.

It is a huge and searching test of our gospel commitment that we recognise that the Lord has his people everywhere, often in what may appear to us the strangest of places. Recognising, accepting, and embracing bothers and sisters in Christ, however different they are from us, was something the Lord Jesus strongly impressed on his disciples. Mark 9:38-41 is one of the most challenging episodes recorded in the Gospels. The disciples saw a man casting out demons in Jesus' name, but they told him to stop, 'because he was not following us'. Jesus immediately rebuked his narrow-hearted disciples, 'Do not stop him.' The disciples could not see beyond themselves. If this man was not one of them he could hardly be one of Christ's. How sad!

The moment we identify the Christian faith with our particular church or denomination or confession of faith, that moment we become a sect and not a true church of Jesus Christ.

None of this means that we are never to try to correct our brothers and sisters and lead them into a richer, more biblical understanding of the faith. No. It does mean that our default is not, 'They need putting right', but, 'These are my family, we are fighting under the same banner, we are heading for the same heavenly country, we are washed in the same blood.' The communion of the saints is a precious and deeply biblical and God-honouring truth. In a justly famous letter to Archbishop Thomas Cranmer, John Calvin wrote:

> This other thing also is to be ranked among the chief evils of our time, viz., that the churches are so divided, that human fellowship is scarcely now

in any repute among us, far less that Christian intercourse which all make a profession of, but few sincerely practise. … Thus it is that the members of the Church being severed, the body lies bleeding. So much does this concern me, that, could I be of any service, I would not grudge to cross even ten seas, if need were, on account of it.[1]

Sometimes family disagreements become public and there may be a good reason why. Most of the time family disagreements remain within the family, and not just because it is never good 'to wash one's dirty linen in public'. More importantly, God's blood-bought children should always want to please their heavenly Father and the Saviour to whom they are united by the Holy Spirit. Like all fathers, our heavenly Father desires to see his children live in harmony.

14. Seventy Thousand Fathoms Deep: The Gospel's Unfathomable Depth

Søren Aabye Kierkegaard, the nineteenth-century Danish philosopher-theologian, described life as paddling in an ocean seventy thousand fathoms deep. How right he was! This thought even more appropriate to the study of theology, the coherent teaching about

[1] John Calvin, *Tracts and Letters*, ed. Jules Bonnet (Edinburgh: Banner of Truth, 2009), V.347-48).

himself that God has revealed to us in the Bible. Some of us know the answer to Question 4 of the *Westminster Shorter Catechism*: 'God is a Spirit, infinite, eternal and unchangeable, etc.' We know the answer, we can parse the sentence, but are we remotely conscious of the depths lying beneath the surface?

We live in an age of pragmatism. We want to know first if something 'works', and if it works, what benefits it will bring to us. This is a trap, a well-laid trap that the Christian church has sadly fallen into, with honourable exceptions. Much church life revolves around doing rather than thinking. I know I am making a false contrast; thinking and doing are not, of course, mutually exclusive. However, activity seems to have become the great business of the modern evangelical church. Our primary thought seems often to be, 'What will attract the people?' Or, 'How can we make our services more user-friendly?' Or, 'How can we make the gospel less objectionable and more appealing?' None of these questions are inherently wrong. But when they become unmoored from the rich depths, 'the seventy thousand fathoms' of the gospel, they become idols that need smashing.

When Paul came to the conclusion of his exposition of 'the gospel of God' in Romans 11:33 he exclaimed, 'Oh, the depth of the riches and wisdom and knowledge of God! How unsearchable are his judgments and how inscrutable his ways!' Paul felt utterly out of his depth. He was like a drowning man who discovered that beneath his feet lay seventy thousand fathoms of rich, mind-expanding, heart-throbbing, overwhelming truth. As I write this I am asking myself, 'Ian, can you remotely feel what the apostle felt? In your life and in your ministry are you conscious, and are others conscious, that beneath you lie seventy thousand fathoms of divine truth?' I wonder.

Too often evangelicals content themselves with gospel sound bites, pithy slogans that catch the mood of our sound-bite culture. My concern is not that we imitate the great doctors of the church (such as Augustine, Calvin, Owen, Edwards, Murray) and mimic them. Rather my concern, first for myself and then for all who read these chapters, is that we stop and reevaluate how we think about God's word and the saving gospel of our Lord Jesus Christ. Do we *think* at all? Do we make time to think? Are we reading 'beyond our understanding'? Does that seem a strange thing to say? What I mean is, are we stretching ourselves intellectually in order that we might sink a little bit more deeply into the seventy thousand fathoms?

Allow me to give you a short list of books that will begin to give you a sense of the seventy thousand fathoms beneath you:

1. *Knowing God* by J. I. Packer, a fine, readable and engaging primer on Christian theology.

2. *Redemption—Accomplished and Applied* by John Murray. This is my all-time favourite paperback; a wonderful exposition of the work of Christ under the rubric of his obedience to his Father.

3. *Jonathan Edwards, A New Biography* by Iain H. Murray. Edwards was an astonishing Christian thinker, preacher, pastor and man. He was one of the greatest thinkers in the history of the church. Murray gives you a sense of the seventy thousand fathoms that Edwards delighted to explore and rejoice in.

4. *The Institutes of the Christian Religion* by John Calvin. This is the greatest exposition of Holy Scripture anywhere at any time (at least I think so). Don't be put off; Calvin is easy to read, if at times too profound to grasp.

5. Last, but not least, *Communion with God*, volume II in the *Collected Works of John Owen* (the Banner of Truth Trust also has a modern version of this remarkable classic in its Puritan Paperback series). When I first read this I felt completely out of my depth.

These are enough to be going on with. Seventy thousand fathoms. Actually, the seventy thousand fathoms are in really an infinite depth. Good plunging!

15. David Martyn Lloyd-Jones: Gospel Preaching in Spirit and Power

One of evangelicalism's buzz words is 'relevance'. If the gospel is to impact our modern, secular, scientific, multi-cultural and multi-faith world, it must show 'relevance'. At one level this is undeniably true. The gospel must always be proclaimed intelligently and imaginatively. We are always to address people as they are and where they are in their thinking and behaving. The gospel is never to be antiquarian, either in the language we use or in the style we adopt. But what exactly does it mean to be 'relevant'?

How are we to 'preach the word' (2 Tim. 4:2) today into a world where Christian truth is at best barely tolerated and at worst violently opposed and mocked? David Martyn Lloyd-Jones (1899–1981) can help us to know how.

The ministry of Martyn Lloyd-Jones, first in Sandfields, South Wales, and then in Westminster Chapel, London, was remarkably blessed and fruitful. His preaching, first among the working-class people of Sandfields and then among the teeming masses of central London, was devoid of 'amusing introductions', lacked the colourful illustrations thought to be so necessary to engaging preaching today, and lasted around fifty minutes. He did not possess a commanding physical presence, and yet he compelled attention. Humanly speaking, 'the Doctor' was no exemplar for young men aspiring to be preachers. And yet his ministry was singularly owned and blessed by God.

The first time I heard the Doctor preach I was nineteen years of age and still finding my feet as a young Christian. An older friend from church asked if I would go with him to hear Dr Lloyd-Jones preach at the centenary of a YMCA in Glasgow. I had only recently heard the name Martyn Lloyd-Jones through the pages of *The Banner of Truth* magazine and knew he was a much-respected preacher. The YMCA hall was full to overflowing. I remember wondering, as I looked at the (to me at least) aged and venerable men on the platform, which one was Dr Lloyd-Jones. It was only when the speaker was introduced and he stood to speak that I saw for the first time the man whose ministry had such a powerfully good impact on the cause of Christ in the United Kingdom and beyond. He was a short man, almost seventy years of age, and recently retired from his long ministry in Westminster Chapel.

I cannot remember how long ML-J preached. I do remember that the time simply flew by. Almost from the moment he opened his mouth to speak, I was hooked. But what was it that hooked me and compelled my attention? I probably then could not have put it into the words I would use today. All I remember was the compelling God-centredness of his preaching. God in Christ was magnified. Later, with a little more knowledge of God's word, I realised I had been in the presence of preaching that was 'in demonstration of the Spirit and of power'.

My first experience echoed that of J. I. Packer. When Packer was a twenty-two-year-old student he heard Lloyd-Jones preach each Sunday evening during the school year of 1948–49. He said that he had 'never heard such preaching'. It came to him 'with the force of an electric shock', giving to him more of a sense of God than any other man he had known.

What was the 'secret' of ML-J's preaching that so arrested and compelled his hearers? The answer, at least the answer the Doctor would give, is: there is no 'secret', other than the 'open secret' of 1 Corinthians 2:1-5! In these verses, the apostle Paul, in contrasting his ministry with the work of the popular philosophers and orators of his day, says: 'and my speech and my message were not in plausible words of wisdom, but in demonstration of the Spirit and of power'. The apostle here uses the strong Greek adversative '*alla*' ('but') to show exactly what his preaching was, and what it was not.

Negatively, it was not 'in plausible words of wisdom'. The power in Paul's preaching did not lie in his oratory, or in his style. In 2 Corinthians 4:2, Paul explains the nature and manner of his preaching ministry: 'we have renounced disgraceful, underhanded ways. We refuse to practise cunning or to tamper with God's word, but by the open statement of the truth we would commend ourselves to everyone's conscience in the sight of God.' Paul was being criticised by some in Corinth for being unimpressive. Put alongside some of the Corinthian orators, Paul lacked style, drama, eloquence. But Paul had never sought to cultivate such things as these. His one concern was by 'open statement of the truth', to commend the gospel of God's grace in Christ to the consciences of his hearers — and to do so 'in demonstration of the Spirit and of power'.

Like Paul, ML-J was his own man. It never crossed his mind to try to impress mere men, or if it did he quickly mortified the thought.

Positively, it was, 'in demonstration of the Spirit and of power'. These words take us to the heart and enduring relevance of ML-J's preaching ministry. He understood, not merely doctrinally but in the depths of his soul, the words of the Lord Jesus Christ, 'apart from me, you can do nothing' (John 15:5). Preaching was not a performance; preaching was a divine encounter, God, through his word and by his Spirit, coming to lay exclusive claim to our hearts and minds and all. For ML-J, preaching was logic, but 'logic on fire'.

In his seminal book *Preaching and Preachers*, ML-J defines somewhat what he meant by the evocative phrase 'logic on fire'. It means being lifted up by the Holy Spirit, 'beyond the efforts and endeavours of man to a position in which the preacher is being used by the Spirit and becomes the channel through whom the Spirit works'.

For ML-J, preaching is theology on fire. Where there is no 'fire', there is no true doctrine and no effective preaching. The reason for this is simple: God's truth is instinct with life. It is God's, the living God's, truth.

In his book *Peter: Eyewitness of His Majesty*, Edward Donnelly has a chapter entitled 'Spirit-filled Preaching', in which he describes the coming of the Spirit on the preaching of God's word:

Most true preachers have had experience of this marvellous enabling. Its coming is unpredictable, often unexpected. Suddenly the minister's heart is aflame and his words seem clothed with a new power. The congregation is strangely hushed or moved. There is a palpable sense of the presence of God. The Spirit exercises a melting, penetrating influence, so that all are aware that momentous issues are before them ... such an experience is unforgettable, addictive, a day of heaven on earth. Once a preacher has known the richness of God's enabling, he can never again rest satisfied without it.[1]

So, how are preachers to preach in demonstration of the Spirit and of power? ML-J would have been the first to tell us that there is nothing formulaic about such preaching. Of course, we must pray and ask. But there is something prior (does this surprise you?):

Do not agonise in prayer, beseeching him for power. Do what he has told you to do. Live the Christian life. Pray, and meditate upon him. Spend time with him and ask him to manifest himself to you. And as long as you do that, you can leave the rest to him. He will give you strength—'as thy days, so shall thy strength be' (Deut. 33:25). He knows us better than we know ourselves, and according to our need

---

[1] Edward Donnelly, *Peter: Eyewitness of His Majesty* (Edinburgh: Banner of Truth Trust, 1998), p. 91.

so will be our supply. Do that and you will be able to say with the Apostle: 'I am able [made strong] for all things through the One who is constantly infusing strength into me.'[1]

I close with words that take me back to my first encounter with the Doctor: 'What is the chief end of preaching? I like to think it is this. It is to give men and women a sense of God and His presence.' What higher goal could gospel preachers aspire to? May the Spirit himself enable us to so preach that it will be manifest to everyone that we preach not ourselves but Jesus Christ as Lord (2 Cor. 4:5), and do so 'in demonstration of the Spirit and of power' (1 Cor. 2:4).

16. The Obedience of Faith: The Gospel Works

P aul's Letter to the Romans is a pastoral *tour de force*. It is of course richly theological. Nowhere does Paul more deeply and beautifully open up to us the gospel of God's saving grace in Christ. But Paul's theology of grace is not an abstract exposition of doctrine. He is concerned to explain to the church in Rome the gospel he preached

[1] D. Martyn Lloyd-Jones, *The Life of Peace: Studies in Philippians 3 and 4* (London: Hodder & Stoughton, 1990), pp. 225-27.

and to establish them in that gospel. The apostle's doctrine always has a pastoral edge to it. True theology is for living; it is never a brute chunk of fact.

That said, it is striking how Paul bookends this Letter to the Romans with an identical phrase, 'the obedience of faith' (1:5 and 16:26). He begins his letter telling the church in Rome that he had 'received grace and apostleship to bring about the obedience of faith for the sake of his [Jesus'] name among all the nations'; and he ends his letter by telling them that God's revelation in the 'prophetic writings' was 'to bring about the obedience of faith' among all nations.

What is 'the obedience of faith'? Faith, self-renouncing trust in Jesus Christ, is obedience to the gospel command to believe on the Lord Jesus Christ for salvation. But it is doubtful if that is quite what 'the obedience of faith' means. More likely, the phrase is used to tell us that faith in Jesus Christ initiates a believer into a life of obedience to Jesus Christ. Where there is no heart obedience to Christ, there can be no saving faith in Christ. This should be obvious to all of us. Faith is not mere notional assent to biblical propositions. Faith—what the Bible means by faith—takes us into Christ, bringing us into living, personal union and communion with Christ.

But Jesus Christ is not held out to us in the gospel only as a Saviour from sin. He is set forth as prophet and king as well as priest. As priest, he made atonement for our sin and now intercedes at God's right hand to bless, defend, and protect us. As prophet, he stands before us as the heavenly Father's last and best word. As king, he rules over us as our sovereign. He has bought us with his own blood and we are not our own (1 Cor. 6:19-20). The threefold offices of Christ impress on us the nature of the salvation that is ours through faith alone in God's Son. He has saved us to be his treasured possession (Exod. 19:5; 1 Pet. 2:9). He has saved us to make us his faithful, loving, obedient servants. We are not our own. We have been saved to glorify God in our bodies.

There is another aspect or dimension to 'the obedience of faith'. The Christian's obedience of Christ is to be a *believing* obedience. All we do we are to do in faith. This is what distinguishes *evangelical* obedience from *legal* obedience. Legal obedience is fuelled by a desire to earn merit with God. It is born of fear not of love. It is duteous without being truly dutiful. In contrast, evangelical obedience is fuelled by love and thankfulness. It is prompted by a desire to please the Saviour. It sees obedience to God's commandments not as an onerous chore, but as a true delight (read Psa. 119:24, 35, 47, 70, 97; John 14:15). Love truly does make obedience sweet.

The obedience of faith. How do our lives measure up? Is our faith a truly biblical and saving faith, that is, a faith that loves and pursues obedience? Is our obedience to Christ fuelled with thankfulness and love? Is our obedience partial and selective? Or is our obedience 'all round'? Do we grieve over our failures in obedience, above all because our failures grieve our beloved Saviour who died that we might live?

It was common in some church circles in years past to say that Jesus could be your Saviour but not your Lord, that first you receive him as Saviour and then, at some later time, receive him as Lord. This thinking led to the astonishing notion that there could be such a thing as a Christian who lived in disobedience to Christ. It is true that all Christians sin and sometimes sin very badly. But if we say that we know Christ but do not keep his commandments, we are liars and the truth is not in us. So said the apostle John (1 John 2:4). One of the 'birthmarks' of a Christian is a heartfelt sorrow and grief over disobedience and a daily resolve, dependent on the Lord, to live more obediently to his commandments.

The Psalmist wrote, 'Oh how I love your law!' (Psa. 119:97). We who live this side of Calvary have even greater cause to say, 'Oh how I love your law!' Do we?

17. Ups and Downs:
The Erratic Nature of the Gospel-Shaped Life

The Christian life is full of extraordinary 'highs' and unsettling 'lows'. This is something for which young Christians are often unprepared. And yet God's word could not be clearer that our spiritual good requires that the Lord lead us through dark valleys as well as lift us up to expansive mountain tops. This is why reading constantly in the Psalms is such a healthy and sobering experience for the child of God. There we encounter faith at its purest, most ardent, most perplexed, most humbled, and most exhilarating.

My point in saying this is to remind you that the life of faith is erratic and irregular, not even and unhindered. John Owen, the great English Puritan divine, makes this point powerfully in his magisterial treatment of sanctification in volume III of his *Works*. He writes: just as 'the growth of plants is not by a constant insensible progress ... but ... by sudden gusts and motions', so 'the growth of believers consists principally in some intense vigorous actings of grace on great occasions'.[1] It has pleased the Lord not to give us steady, uninterrupted growth in grace; rather, he is pleased to have us cry to him, wait on him, seek his face, often in the midst of trials, before he grants us to grow in likeness to the Saviour—if nothing else, to humble us, and keep us dependent on him. If our Lord Jesus is the proto-typical man of faith (and he is), then the pattern of his life will be the essential pattern of our lives. What the Spirit first produced in him he comes to reproduce in us. And what was the pattern of the Saviour's earthly life? Was it even and untroubled? No. He was brought by

[1] *Works*, III.397.

his Father through dark valleys, where, the writer to the Hebrews tells us, he 'learned obedience through what he suffered' (Heb. 5:8).

In the light of this, Owen anticipates a pressing pastoral question: 'I do not see much, if any, growth in grace in my life: am I therefore devoid of the root of holiness?' Owen's response is measured, searching, and pastorally reassuring. He says:

> every one in whom is a principle of spiritual life, who is born of God, in whom the work of sanctification is begun, if it be not gradually carried on in him, if he thrive not in grace and holiness, if he go not from strength to strength, it is ordinarily from his own sinful negligence.[1]

Owen urges us then to search our hearts if we appear to be regressing in holiness, and to cast off the sin that so easily besets us. Self-examination, in the light of God's great grace to us in Christ, is a necessity. Without it we can so easily drift into spiritual presumption and self-deception.

But Owen proceeds quickly to balance what he has just said. It is one thing for holiness to be present and another for the believer to be conscious of it. Indeed, continues Owen, 'there may be seasons wherein sincere, humble believers may be obliged to believe the increase and growth of [holiness] in them when they perceive it not, so as to be

---

[1] *Ibid.*, p. 400.

sensible of it'.[1] Owen never forgets he is a pastor, writing for Christ's lambs. He is quick to reassure struggling saints: 'What shall we say, then? Is there no sincere holiness where … decays are found? God forbid.'[2] Progress is erratic and 'horticultural', not steady and 'mechanical'.

Owen is not soft-peddling sin in the believer. He is not condoning lack of godly resolve. He is, however, recognising that the life of faith is inherently erratic, horticultural in its growth and development and not mechanical.

My main concern in writing this is to encourage you to do one thing—*read the Psalms*. Read them daily. Be constantly refreshed, humbled, and reassured by them. Learn the shape of the life of faith—not least to guard you from being beguiled by the temptation to seek shortcuts to holiness. I want to assure you of one thing: reading the Psalms will not leave you content with the state of your Christian life. They will unsettle you, as well as encourage you. They will lift you into the heights, but at times draw you into the depths. John Calvin wisely said of the Psalms that they are an 'anatomy of all the parts of the soul'. See yourself in the Psalms. But more importantly, see Christ there, leading you onwards and upwards—though the 'upwards' may at times be discovered in the 'downwards'. Does that make sense to you?

[1] *Ibid.*, p. 401.
[2] *Ibid.*

18. *Living by the Means of Grace: How We Grow Up in the Gospel (1)*

God's ultimate purpose concerns the glory of his Son, not the beautifying of his children. God is intent on beautifying his redeemed children but this is his *proximate*, not his *ultimate* purpose. God's ultimate purpose is to conform his children to the likeness of his Son in order to make him 'the firstborn among many brothers' (Rom. 8:29). The heavenly Father's first priority does not terminate on you or on me, but on his beloved Son.

Romans 8:29 makes it absolutely clear that Jesus Christ is the essence, the epitome, and the ultimate paradigm of the beauty to which God seeks to conform all his children. He alone is 'altogether lovely' (Song of Sol. 5:16 KJV). I need hardly tell you that the Saviour's beauty is pre-eminently moral and spiritual, not physical. At the very moment that 'he had no form or majesty ... no beauty that we should desire him' (Isa. 53:2), he was 'altogether lovely'. The beauty of the Saviour that pervaded and shone through his humanity was nothing less than the moral glory of God. When the Lord brings us to the new birth, the birth from above, he plants within our yet sinful lives his 'seed' (1 John 3:9), what one old writer called the 'life of God in the soul of man'. God's purpose in saving sinners is not only to save them but to sanctify them, to transform them into the likeness of his Son.

Colossians 3:12-16 is a magnificent and deeply humbling portrait of the child of God. This is Jesus, the perfect elect Servant-Son of the Father. This is what the elect of God are to look like. Is this what you look like? Is this what the church to which we belong looks like? What power and credibility such beauty would give to our evangelism!

It is God's ultimate purpose to exalt his Son and to make all his blood-bought, redeemed children like his Son to conform us to the beauty of his likeness.

But how does God go about the work of conforming us to the likeness of his Son, of 'beautifying his children'?

We need, first, to be absolutely clear that there is no one experience, no matter how deep and profound and transformative, that perfectly beautifies God's children. We must learn instinctively to avoid like the plague all second-blessing theologies and experiences. Every Christian is summoned to 'grow in the grace and knowledge of our Lord and Saviour Jesus Christ' (2 Pet. 3:18). I wonder if Peter had in his mind the words of Luke 2:40, 52? Our Saviour's growth, of course, was not from imperfection to perfection, but from one degree of glory to another (see also Heb. 5:8). But our growth is from imperfection to perfection; but perfection will not be attained until our lowly bodies are transformed to be like his glorious body at Christ's coming (Phil. 3:20-21). Christian beauty, likeness to Christ, doesn't just 'happen' (cf. Phil. 3:13-14). Paul applied himself with relentless, single-minded determination 'toward the goal for the prize of the upward call of God in Christ Jesus'. Paul was a 'one-thing-I-do' man. Are you a 'one-thing-I-do' person? Is it your daily resolve to grow in the grace and knowledge of your Lord and Saviour Jesus Christ? It will not just happen. Peter exhorts us to give *all diligence* to add to our faith (2 Pet. 1:5 KJV), and Paul summons us to *work out* our own salvation with fear and trembling, always knowing that it is God who works in us both to will and to do of his good pleasure (Phil. 2:12-13).

That being said, Christians grow up in the gospel supremely, but not only, by the 'ordinary means of grace' (which are actually 'extraordinary'). I say 'supremely but not only'. Why? For this reason: God works all things together for the good of his children (Rom. 8:28). God presses all of life into his service as means of grace. I am conscious that our Reformation heritage has stressed (and rightly so) the 'ordinary means of grace', the preaching, hearing, and reading of God's word, the sacraments of baptism and the Lord's Supper, prayer (both corporate and private), and godly discipline. But there is a danger to avoid here: the danger of thinking that growth in grace is tied to those formally-ordained means of grace. In Romans 8:28, we are reminded that 'all things' are means of grace to God's children as he wisely, sovereignly, gloriously, and mysteriously bends them to the beautifying of his children.

There is an ocean of encouragement for us in these words. All of life is bent by God and shaped by God and invaded by God to secure the good of his people. God's

sovereign providence is one of the great anchors that sup-
ports and keeps the souls of believers. Anchors will not
keep you from being buffeted and battered by storms,
but they do keep you from being swept off course! Every
incident and circumstance in life can be a means of grace in
the kind providence of God as we submit to and embrace
his ever-wise purposes. God is personally and actively
involved in every detail of his children's lives, pursuing the
holiness of his people. Your growth in grace is not tied to
those occasions when the word and the sacraments and
prayer are corporately and consciously engaged in. In 'all
things' God works for the good of those who love him,
those who are called according to his purpose.

19. Living by the Means of Grace: How We Grow Up in the Gospel (2)

In an age of unbridled individualism among evangelical Christians, we need to be reminded often of the
centrality and importance of the church in the economy
of God. We are so unconsciously infected by the incipient
and strident individualism of the age that many Christians
no longer instinctively think in corporate and covenantal terms (cf. Eph. 3:19). The church is the supreme (if
not the only) context in which the means of grace oper-

ate. Working through the Spirit, and by his word, God uses the means of grace for the gathering in of his elect and their subsequent edification and sanctification. To that end the risen Lord has endowed his church with all kinds of spiritual gifts, and given to it offices or ministries for the preaching of the word, the administration of the sacraments, and the exercise of godly discipline (Eph. 4:7-13), 'for the perfecting of the saints' (Eph 4:12 KJV).

Paul is highlighting the truth that the church, the local covenant fellowship, is the supreme locus for the exposition of those gifts that are means of grace.

The significance of the church with respect to the sanctifying of the elect was a dominant theme in the writings of the magisterial Reformers. Listen to Calvin as he begins his exposition of the church:

> I shall start, then, with the church, into whose bosom God is pleased to gather his sons, not only that they may be nourished by her help and ministry ... but also that they may be guided by her motherly care until they mature and at last reach the goal of faith ... so that, for those to whom he is Father the church may also be Mother.[1]

In his *Commentary on Ephesians* he makes the same point: 'The Church is the common mother of all the godly,

[1] *Institutes* IV.i.1. Calvin is, of course, consciously echoing Cyprian, 'You cannot have God for your Father unless you have the church for your Mother.' The Reformers were more than happy to endorse, rightly understood, the Patristic aphorism, '*Extra ecclesiam nulla salus*'!

which bears, nourishes, and governs in the Lord both kings and commoners; and this is done by the ministry.'[1] Calvin is simply echoing the teaching of God's word. The great means of grace are located within the fellowship and ministry of Christ's church.

Calvin doesn't mean, and I don't mean, that Christians should not cultivate individual and familial communion with God. But rather, he is asking, Do we give to the church the place it ought to have in our lives? Are we devoted to its fellowship? Its ministry? Its purity? Its God-ordained centrality? Are you like the Psalmist who said, 'I was glad when they said to me, "Let us go to the house of the LORD"' (Psa. 122:1)?

This corporate, covenantal note was imbedded in the life of Christ's church from the beginning. It was a striking feature of old covenant religion. It was a striking feature at the inception of new covenant religion too (Acts 2:42). The fellowship of the saints, God's church, was prized and cherished. The early Christians 'devoted themselves' to the 'fellowship'. The church was the people of God, and it was the 'holy temple', the holy place in which God dwelt by his Spirit (see Eph. 2:21-22; 1 Cor. 3:16-17). This basic, yet deeply profound biblical truth not only honours the one institution established by our Lord Jesus Christ, it also helps us to resist the atomising, fragmenting mindset that so bedevils evangelical Christianity in this present

---

[1] See on Eph. 4:12.

age. Reformation Christianity not only magnified the justifying grace and imputed righteousness that becomes the possession of every believing sinner, it laboured to set that justifying grace in its biblical, that is to say, corporate and covenantal, context. Justifying grace not only brings you into saving union with Christ; it brings you into the fellowship of his body, the church.

20. Living by the Means of Grace: How We Grow Up in the Gospel (3)

It is a Reformed truism that God's usual, if not invariable, means for beautifying his children is the ministry of his living, powerful, wise, good, and infallible word. It is the word preached, made visible in the sacraments, applied to the life of the church, and voiced in Spirit-inspired prayer, that the Holy Spirit uses to make us more like our Lord Jesus Christ. More particularly, what the Holy Spirit first produced in Christ, he comes in his new covenant ministry to reproduce in the people of Christ. This is what John Calvin called the Spirit's ministry of 'replication'.

To appreciate the Spirit's sanctifying ministry in believers through the word, we need first to appreciate his sanctifying ministry in Christ through the word.

Jesus and the word of God

The New Testament tells us that our Lord's sanctification was both *definitive* and *progressive*. We read in Luke 1:35: 'The Holy Spirit will come upon you, and the power of the Most High will overshadow you; therefore the child to be born will be called holy—the Son of God.' From his mother's womb, as no other, Jesus was 'holy, innocent, unstained, separated from sinners' (Heb. 7:26). But Luke also tells us that 'Jesus increased in wisdom and in stature and in favour with God and man' (Luke 2:52). He 'increased in wisdom' just as he 'learned obedience ... being made perfect' (Heb. 5:8-9).

If we were now to ask the question, 'But how did Jesus increase in wisdom and learn obedience and become perfect'?, the Bible's answer is clear: Jesus did so by living under the word of God. See Isaiah 50:4-5. As the Lord's Servant, Jesus lived 'under the word'. He describes himself as a Servant who had been 'taught': 'Morning by morning he awakens; he awakens my ear to hear as those who are taught.' The Lord God has opened his ear. And because he has been 'taught' he knows 'how to sustain with a word him who is weary'. Notice what is being said here: 'the Lord GOD has opened my ear'. As the Servant of the Lord, our covenant head in our frail flesh, he needed the Lord to open his ears to hear! The word of God was absolutely instrumental in the developing sanctification of our Lord Jesus.

When Jesus was tempted by the devil in the wilderness, what did he do? See Luke 4:4, 8, 12. Three times Jesus brought to mind words, pertinent and powerful words, found in Deuteronomy 8:3; 6:13; 6:16. How was he able to do this? How did Jesus acquire this knowledge of the word of God? Was it immediately and indelibly impressed on his DNA while in the womb? If so, then his humanity is not our humanity! The human nature he took to himself was not created *ex nihilo*, but was inherited through Mary. It was *our* human nature, 'addicted to so many wretchednesses', as Calvin so vividly puts it, that the Saviour took to himself.[1] No, just as he 'learned obedience', so he 'learned the word of God'. His mind and heart were so saturated with the word of God that he was able immediately to bring that word to mind and repulse the devil's temptations.

Now here is the key thing: What the Spirit first produced in Christ, he comes by his ministry of replication to produce in his people.

Consider three texts

John 17:17: 'Sanctify them in the truth; your word is truth.' Jesus is praying that his Father's truth, his living word, would shape and sanctify his disciples. But, as Robert Dabney comments, 'truth has no adequate efficiency to sanctify by itself … yet it has a natural adaptation to be the means of sanctification in the hands of the Holy Ghost'.[2]

---

[1] *Comm.* on John 1:14.
[2] Robert L. Dabney, *Lectures in Systematic Theology* (1871; repr. Edinburgh: Banner of Truth Trust, 1985), p. 665.

Psalm 119:11: 'I have stored up your word in my heart, that I might not sin against you.' Now the Psalmist could hardly be saying that the mere remembrance of God's word, in its syllables and syntax, could keep him from sin. It is that word applied and blessed to us by the mortifying and vivifying ministry of the Holy Spirit that keeps us from sin.

Psalm 119:18: 'Open my eyes, that I may behold wondrous things out of your law.' Here we see two things: First, the Psalmist's *faith*: every exercise in the believer's life is to be an exercise of faith. The Psalmist is acknowledging his dependence on the covenant Lord to give him true understanding, and he does so as a believer! When God makes us new creations in Christ he does not plant within us a lifetime of unaided understanding. Rather, he gives us his Holy Spirit, the Spirit of the risen, exalted Jesus Christ, and he would have us come to him day by day in believing dependence, just as the Saviour did in the frailty of our flesh!

Second, the Psalmist's *humility*. He does not content himself with his standing before God, with his past insights, with his divinely appointed office. He comes to the word of God in a spirit of personal humility before God. The natural abilities and divine gifts given to the Psalmist are no guarantee that he will be able to understand the mind of God!

John Owen, the English Puritan pastor-theologian, put the matter memorably: 'He that would utterly separate the Spirit from the word had as good burn his Bible. The bare letter of the New Testament will no more ingenerate faith and obedience in the souls of men ... than the letter of the Old Testament doth so at this day among the Jews.'[1] He makes the same point in his famous work on the mortification of sin: 'All ways and means without [the Holy Ghost] are as a thing of naught.'[2] Owen is only saying what the word of God itself says (1 Cor. 2:9-12). If I were given a book on advanced calculus, I would know the book was about calculus (I can read!). I could even at one time make a little sense of elementary integration and differentiation; but the internal coherence of the book, its fundamental premises, its considered conclusions, its remarkable applications to life, would all escape me. I need someone who understands calculus from the inside to explain it to me (cf. Acts 8:30-38).

The sanctifying work of God comes to us by his word and Spirit, through faith. Wilhelmus à Brakel, the experiential Dutch theologian, wrote:

> It is there [in the word of God] that sins are held forth in their abominable nature and spiritual life is revealed in its desirability. Scripture convicts, rebukes, threatens, and judges. It contains exhortations and various inducements, Christ is presented as the Fountain of sanctification, and it contains the promises. All this the Holy Spirit applies to the

[1] *Works*, III.192-93.
[2] *Works*, VI.41.

heart of believers, exercising and activating them unto sanctification—the word of God being an instrument in the hand of God (apart from which a means cannot be operative).[1]

21. *Living by the Means of Grace:*
How We Grow up in the Gospel (4)

The Lord gave us his sacraments, wrote Calvin, 'to sustain the weakness of our faith'. The sacraments are divine accommodations to our sinful weakness. In a wonderfully vivid and beautifully written passage, Calvin says:

> But as our faith is slight and feeble unless it be propped up on all sides and sustained by every means, it trembles, wavers, totters, and at last gives way. Here our merciful Lord, according to his infinite kindness, so tempers himself to our capacity that, since we are creatures who always creep on the ground, cleave to the flesh, and do not think about or conceive of anything spiritual, he condescends to lead us to himself even by these earthly elements, and to set before us in the flesh a mirror of spiritual blessings.[2]

[1] Wilhelmus à Brakel, *The Christian's Reasonable Service* (Grand Rapids: Reformation Heritage Books, 1994), III.5.

[2] *Institutes* IV.xiv.3.

While this is no doubt true, it is surely no less true that the sacraments are also adapted to our humanity *per se*. Calvin himself seems to acknowledge this. Quoting Chrysostom, he recognises that it is 'because we have souls engrafted in bodies [that] he imparts spiritual things under visible ones'.[1] This suggests that the sacraments are not merely gracious 'accommodations' to our sinful capacities; more properly, perhaps, they are gracious accommodations to our intrinsic humanity. In the garden, the Lord gave Adam a tree to confirm and make visible to him his promise (and threat).

At a time when Reformed churches are taking the celebration and frequency of the Lord's Supper more seriously, the question 'How should I benefit from communion?' is timely. I want, however, to make a small but significant change to the question just posed. The change appears minimal, but it is actually profound. I would like to substitute the plural pronoun '*we*' for the singular '*I*'.

Christians too easily, and unbiblically, think of the Christian life purely in personal, singular categories. We read the Bible as if it were addressed particularly to us as individuals, when, in fact, it was written to God's people in their corporate, covenantal identity. I do not mean for one moment that the Christian faith is not personal, or that there is no such thing as individual faith. Indeed, 'the Son of God ... loved *me* and gave himself for *me*' (Gal. 2:20).

[1] *Ibid.*

Rather, my point is this: God's people are one. Salvation brings us into the one body of Christ, his church (1 Cor. 12:13). The default mode for the Christian life, then, is not 'me and Jesus', but 'us and Jesus'. The Lord's Prayer puts it memorably: 'When you pray, say: "*Our* Father … ."' With this in mind let us think a little about our question.

John Calvin begins his exposition of the sacraments with these words: 'We have in the sacraments another aid to our faith related to the preaching of the gospel.'[1] The key words here are 'aid to our faith'. In giving us sacraments, Calvin goes on to say, 'God provides first for our ignorance and dullness, then for our weakness.' The sacraments are needed, not because God's word is lacking in any way, but because we need all the help God can give us to instruct us and establish us in the faith of our Lord Jesus Christ.

This is our starting point. We have a kind and merciful God who uses earthly elements 'to lead us to himself'. All the benefits we are to receive from partaking of the Supper will be experienced in God leading us to himself. He wants his children to know him better. The Lord's Supper is a gracious gift from a gracious Saviour to help us better grasp and experience his love for us.

The first thing that needs to be affirmed, then, is that believers are expected to benefit from participation in the Lord's Supper. The Lord has not left us a spectacle for us to admire, but a Supper for us to eat and by which we are

---

[1] *Institutes* IV.xv.1.

to be spiritually nourished. Just as we give our children food to nourish them, so the Lord has given his children food to nourish them. Along with the preaching, hearing, and reading of God's word, prayer and the fellowship of the saints, the sacraments are 'means of grace'. They are not bare or empty symbols, but vehicles for the Holy Spirit to bring us into sweeter communion with our risen Saviour (cf. 1 Cor. 10:16). We benefit from the Supper as we recognise and receive Christ by faith in the emblems of bread and wine.

Second, any benefit that we are to obtain from feeding on Christ at the Supper is dependent, in large measure, on grasping that we are feeding on Christ in communion with other believers. The Lord's Supper is not a transaction first between the individual Christian and Christ, but between the church fellowship as a whole and Christ.

This is highlighted graphically and dramatically in 1 Corinthians 10:17. The one common loaf is an expression of, indeed a symbol of, the one people of God. In other words, we gather at the Supper as 'family'. We are there together to meet with and to hold fellowship with our risen Lord. I am not at all saying that there is no individual benefit for believers at the Supper. Rather, I am saying that we come to the Lord's Table not as a disparate group of like-minded and like-hearted believers, but as God's one family. This means that we must seek to cultivate a sense of the theological imperative at the heart of the Supper, *viz.* that it heralds, highlights, and proclaims the oneness of Christ's church, the unity of the twice-born. Just as a family is greater than its constituent parts, so the church is greater than an aggregate of its members.

One of Paul's solemn strictures on the Corinthian church was that people were eating and drinking 'without waiting for anybody else' (1 Cor. 11:21 NIV). There was an arrogant individualism that was bringing great dishonour to the celebrating of the Lord's Supper.

Two practical points may help us derive benefit from the Supper: First, *think familially*. As you eat and drink say to yourself, 'These are my brothers and sisters. We are all one in Christ. We belong to one another. We have all been redeemed by the same blood and are indwelt by the same Spirit. We are all the children of the same Father. We are blessed beyond all words.' Second, it will also help if we placard our unity by *eating and drinking together*, not individually the moment we receive the bread and wine.

Third, the benefit we receive from eating the Lord's Supper lies, in measure, in understanding what exactly the Supper is. There is the widespread view that the Supper is merely and only a 'memorial' of Christ: 'Do this in remembrance of me.'

It is undeniable that the Supper is a memorial of Christ. We eat and drink in remembrance of him whose body was broken and whose blood was shed for us. It is, however, no less undeniable that the Supper is more than a mere memorial. It is, as Paul dramatically puts it, a 'participation in the blood of Christ' and 'a participation in the body of

Christ' (1 Cor. 10:16). Calvin again takes us to the heart of the matter:

> the signs are bread and wine, which represent for us the invisible food that we receive from the flesh and blood of Christ. ... Now Christ is the only food of our soul, and therefore our Heavenly Father invites us to Christ, that, refreshed by partaking of him, we may repeatedly gather strength until we shall have reached heavenly immortality.[1]

We are not to imagine that the Lord's Supper initiates us into a communion with Christ that we do not have through hearing the word of the gospel in faith. No. 'Since, however, this mystery of Christ's secret union with the devout is by nature incomprehensible, he shows its figure and image in visible signs best adapted to our small capacity.' It is as if our heavenly Father draws us pictures of his grace in Christ to us, so that we will the better grasp and experience the wonder of that grace. Listen again to how Calvin explains this:

> the Sacrament does not cause Christ to begin to be the bread of life; but when it reminds us that he was made the bread of life, which we continually eat, and which gives us a relish and savour of that bread, it causes us to feel the power of that bread.[2]

---

[1] *Institutes* IV.xvii.1.
[2] *Ibid.*, IV.xvii.5.

All of this is a great mystery to us. Calvin even urges us 'not to confine [our] mental interest within ... too narrow limits, but to strive to rise much higher' than he is able to lead us. In a striking statement, he acknowledges,

> although my mind can think beyond what my tongue can utter, yet even my mind is conquered and overwhelmed by the greatness of the thing. Therefore, nothing remains but to break forth in wonder at this mystery, which plainly neither the mind is able to conceive nor the tongue to confess.[1]

The old Scot's saying puts it well: 'It is better felt than telt.' Not everything in the life of faith can be reduced to comprehensive statements. There are profundities that take us out of our depth—and the holy Supper of our Saviour is one of those profundities.

Pray then that the Lord, by the power of his Spirit, will feed you with himself. Pray that his won graces will be more powerfully impressed on your soul. Pray that the presence of the one who walks among the lampstands (see Rev. 1:13, 20; 2:1) will be felt and experienced as in faith we eat his flesh and drink his blood (John 6:53-54).

[1] *Ibid.*, IV.xvii.7.

22. *Living by the Means of Grace: How We Grow Up in the Gospel (5)*

It is a fact of history that the most Christlike Christians are the most prayerful Christians. Why should that be? For this simple reason: you become like the people you live with and love! Have you not noticed that? Prayer is communion with God. It is a spiritual grace.

The early chapters of Acts reveal God's people constantly at prayer: 'All these with one accord were devoting themselves to prayer … And they devoted themselves to the prayers … And … they lifted their voices together to God and said, "Sovereign Lord …"' (Acts 1:14; 2:42; 4:24). Prayer was fundamental not marginal, it was central not supplemental to the life of the early church. Was it not this heartfelt sense of their dependence on God that gave such lustre to the witness of these early believers?

Throughout his letters, Paul enjoined the churches to pray; not as a mere formal spiritual exercise, but as the mark of their sense of creaturely dependence on the grace and sovereign power of God. More than anything else, the example of our Lord Jesus should impress on us the sanctifying power of prayer. He lived a life of prayer. He taught his disciples to pray. He commanded all God's people to pray (Matt. 7:7-11). The pulse beat of his life was prayerful dependence on his Father and the enabling of the Holy Spirit.

In prayer, and as our prayers are informed by God's word, our desires become aligned with God's desires. His thoughts become our thoughts. In this way, likeness to the Saviour becomes an ever-developing feature of our lives.

One of the most significant passages in the Bible's teaching on prayer is Psalm 106. The Psalm celebrates the Lord's remarkable rescuing kindnesses to his covenant people Israel, and details his people's disdain of his great mercies to them. It is hard to take in the persistent cavalier behaviour of Israel in the glowing light of God's repeated mercies in delivering them from their enemies and providing for all their needs in times of deepest trial. Tragically, the psalmist tells us, 'They made a calf in Horeb and worshiped a metal image. They exchanged the glory of God for the image of an ox that eats grass. They forgot God, their Saviour, who had done great things in Egypt' (Psa. 106:19-21). If the Psalmist hadn't written it, we wouldn't have believed it. However, it is what the Psalmist next writes that is especially stunning: 'Therefore he said he would destroy them—had not Moses, his chosen one, stood in the breach before him, to turn away his wrath from destroying them.' God's covenant people were on the edge of extinction. Their repeated wickedness so provoked the Lord that 'he said he would destroy them'.

I have no intention to try to reconcile God's revealed will and his secret counsel, or to spend any time discussing whether God actually changes his mind ('I the LORD do not change' [Mal. 3:6]). I simply want to notice with you how Moses 'stood in the breach before [God] to turn away his wrath from destroying them'. Moses prayed, and God's holy and just wrath was turned away from his wayward, disobedient, and unthankful people. Prayer effected a great change in the fortunes of God's visible church in the world. Moses prayed.

John Bunyan famously wrote, 'You can do more than pray *after* you have prayed, but you cannot do more than pray *until* you have prayed.' In God's great mercy, prayer truly is a means of grace. Not prayer *per se*, of course. It is not prayer, but God who makes the difference, who effects the change. But prayer, believing, intercessory, constant, pleading prayer, is one of the great means God is pleased to use to advance his kingdom and grow his church. One man prayed and a church-nation was blessed and preserved from God's holy anger.

The visible church of God in our world is a pathetic shadow of what it is called to be. There are, thankfully, glorious exceptions. But generally, wherever you look, unbelief, moral compromise, theological downgrade, and social shallowness prevail. The church is so bent on 'relevance' and 'modernity' (the buzz words) that it cannot see just how pathetic it appears to onlookers. It is often little more than a religious mirror image of the world it is called to evangelise—mimicking its values, celebrating its causes. Yes, we can protest. Yes, we must proclaim. But first we must pray.

Above all we must pray concertedly as churches. The early Christians devoted themselves to prayer, as a body (Acts 2:42). Corporate prayer was woven into their lifestyle as Christians. Corporate, congregational prayer was not for a few especially enthusiastic Christians. The whole community of believers 'devoted themselves to … the prayers'. It was inconceivable that truly converted people would not make every effort to be present when the church gathered to pray. The commitment to corporate prayer is underscored by the strength of the verb Luke uses: 'devoted'. It was not merely a matter of turning up, of duteously doing what was expected. These early Christians *devoted* themselves to the prayers. The verb signals the religious commitment of these believers to the set times of prayer (no doubt arranged by the apostles).

We have no way of knowing the precise mechanics of the *when*, the *where*, or even the *how* of these times of prayer. What we do know is that those who were added to the church (Acts 2:41) made the church's times of prayer a non-negotiable priority in their lives, as much as God's providences would enable them.

It is understood that family circumstances and work commitments may mean, at times, that the church's set times of prayer have to be missed. But the fundamental issue is not the hindrances of providence, but the unconcern of our hearts and the distractions of 'other things', even good things. Perhaps by now you are saying to yourself, 'You don't realise how pressed I am, how

many family commitments I have, how much I need time
to spend with my wife, my husband, my children.' Don't I?

Life in general, and your life and mine in particular,
are shaped by priorities, conscious and sub-conscious. We
make time for what we think is important. For our first-
century Christian brothers and sisters, faced as they were
with hostility and severe persecution, corporate prayer
was a top priority. There is a manifest connection in the
early chapters of Acts between the church at prayer and
the church advancing in the power of God. Gospel life is
not neglectful of church prayer meetings.

23. *Living by the Means of Grace: How We Grow Up in the Gospel (6)*

It may seem strange to some people that church discipline could ever contribute to the furtherance of
the gospel and the beautifying of God's children, but in
the hands of the Holy Spirit, ministered with grace, and
received in humility, it does. Church discipline is commanded by God in his word and is to reflect his discipline
of his children: 'For the Lord disciplines the one he loves,
and chastises every son whom he receives' (Heb. 12:6,
quoting Prov. 3:12). And why does the Lord do this?
That 'we may share his holiness' and yield 'the peaceful
fruit of righteousness' (Heb. 12:10-11).

Some years ago the elders in the congregation I served in Cambridge interviewed a young student for membership. When asked why she wanted to be a member of Cambridge Presbyterian Church she replied, 'I was present when the church disciplined a church member for ungodly behaviour, and I thought I wanted to belong to a church that took the honour of God that seriously.' I and my fellow elders were speechless with thankfulness to God.

Yes, church discipline can be, and sadly has been, exercised harshly, unfeelingly, and clinically. But when exercised in love, under the clear teaching of God's word, its purpose is to humble morally and doctrinally wayward believers and bring the church into a new sense of the loving-kindness, holiness, and tender mercy of God, giving godly power to its gospel testimony.

The church in Corinth was awash with divisions, immoral behaviour and doctrinal aberrations. There was even someone in the church practising a form of sexual immorality that was 'not tolerated even among pagans' (1 Cor. 5:1). Paul was appalled that, instead of grieving over behaviour that was bringing public dishonour to Christ and removing this man from the church's fellowship, the church's leaders were doing nothing (1 Cor. 5:2). It seems that the sexual promiscuity that was part of life in Corinth had infected the thinking of some in the church. The gospel calling of believers to live godly, moral, Christ-honouring lives was being compromised by the church turning a blind eye to this man's deeply aberrant behaviour.

Paul's response was unequivocal. First, he rebuked the church for doing nothing. Second, he commanded the church to deliver the man over 'to Satan for the destruction of the flesh, so that his spirit may be saved in the day of the Lord' (1 Cor. 5:5). Paul was not expressing a personal opinion; he was exercising his God-given authority as an apostle of Christ. What we need to notice is that church discipline was to be practised, not neglected, and that the discipline had an ultimately remedial purpose. The aim of church discipline is never to lord it over any man or woman's conscience. The aim is always to seek the present and eternal good of those inside and those outside the church.

God takes sin seriously. The cross of Christ is the ultimate revelation of what God thinks of sin. But we live in a world which either glosses over sin's seriousness or denies it is serious at all. Sadly, but almost inevitably, this thinking seeps its way into the life of the church. God has planted his church as an outpost of heaven in the midst of this fallen world. He has called and commanded us to go and make disciples of all the nations (Matt. 28:18-20). What gives huge credibility to the church's mission and to individual believers' witness is that we live distinctively different lives from those in the world around us, as we shine as lights in a dark world (Phil. 2:15).

The church in Corinth needed to wake up to its responsibility to 'judge' those 'inside the church' (1 Cor. 5:12). The verb Paul uses has the basic idea of 'to discriminate'.

He is not advocating that a judgmental spirit prevail in the church. He is summoning the church to recognise that 'a little leaven leavens the whole lump' (1 Cor. 5:6). Give sin an inch and it will take the proverbial mile. Church discipline has nothing to do with being 'holier than thou'. It has everything to do with having a zeal for God's honour and the effective proclamation of the gospel. The virtual abandonment of church discipline in the modern church reflects the fact that God's honour and the promotion of the gospel are not the priorities and passions they were in the New Testament church.

Are you living by the means of grace? Is your church living by the means of grace? There are no shortcuts to godliness, to the likeness of Christ who is the essence and epitome of godliness. Use all the ordained means God has given to you. Cherish every opportunity to gather with God's people. Prize the unity and peace of Christ's church, which is the soil that nourishes the means of grace. Resist the temptation to separate yourself from the church because of its failures. God is long-suffering towards his church and we are called to be 'imitators of God' (Eph 5:1).

24. *Living in a Fallen World: Practising the Gospel*

The Bible is full of remarkable statements. One of the most remarkable is found in 1 Peter 2:17. Peter is instructing Christians how to live in an essentially godless, anti-Christian society. He writes, 'Honour everyone. Love the brotherhood. Fear God. Honour the emperor.' This is surely remarkable. 'Love the brotherhood' and 'fear God' we can readily understand; but 'honour everyone' and especially 'the emperor'? The emperor in question was probably Nero, the fanatically anti-Christian megalomaniac. Honour *him*? God's word can be deeply unsettling.

You do not need much imagination to see how relevant Peter's words are to Christians in the western world today. We live in an increasingly hostile, anti-Christian, really anti-Christ, society. Christian values are trampled on and Christian beliefs mocked and penalised. It is not fanciful to believe that in the near future, preachers will be arrested for proclaiming the absolute uniqueness of Jesus Christ as Lord and Saviour, and for teaching the moral duties of God's word. Thus it was, and worse, in the days when Peter wrote, 'Honour everyone. Honour the emperor.'

This leaves us asking the question, How are Christians to live today in post-Christian, anti-Christian Britain, USA, or wherever?

First, we are to live humbly confident that the Lord God omnipotent reigns. I don't mean, of course, that we should not grieve deeply over the tragic state of our nation. Nor do I mean that Christians should not repent and cry out to the Lord. With Daniel we should always be saying, 'Lord, we have sinned and done that which is evil in your sight.' But, in the midst of our moral and spiritual tragedies, our God reigns. He has not been caught unawares by the sin that scars the face of our nation. Wonderfully, if mysteriously to us, he ordains all that comes to pass and does so sinlessly, wisely, and purposefully. God's sovereignty is a gloriously comforting truth.

Second, we are to live absolutely assured that the Saviour will not lose one of the sheep for whom he died. Nothing and no one can hinder our Lord Jesus from saving and bringing safely to glory his blood-bought bride. Is this not a glorious truth, a reassuring truth, and, above all, a cause to praise our God no matter the circumstances that defile and deface our nation?

Third, we are to live seeing the enemies of God and the gospel as men and women God loves and holds out his arms to save. God takes no pleasure in the death of the wicked (Ezek. 33:11). He even pleads with them to lay aside their enmity, to repent and come to his Son, Jesus Christ. God is rich in mercy and so also must his people be. We are to love our enemies and do them good and not harm. We are to pray for them and go out of our way to win them to Christ.

Fourth, we are to live remembering that we were all once children of God's wrath like the rest of mankind, until he had mercy on us (Eph. 2:3-4). You and I were once dead in trespasses and sins. We were blinded by the God of this world to the light of the gospel of the glory of God in Christ.

Fifth, we are to live remembering that it is God the sovereign Lord who raises up and who brings down. Donald Trump and Vladimir Putin are where they are not ultimately because they were voted into power, but because the living God appointed them to their respective positions. The Most High God rules in the kingdoms of men, so the Bible assures us (Dan. 4:32). History is not ultimately shaped by the wicked deeds of bad men, though they are absolutely culpable for their actions. But behind the wicked deeds of bad men 'a deeper magic' is at work (for those of you who know C. S. Lewis).

25. De Servo Arbitrio: Gospel Humbling Words

In 1524, Desiderius Erasmus, probably the foremost classical scholar in Europe, published a little book with the title *Diatribe sue collatio de libero arbitrio* (*Discussion Concerning Free Will*). Erasmus wrote the book to distance himself from the teachings of Martin Luther that were setting Europe ablaze and challenging the foundations of the papacy. Erasmus was in the semi-Pelagian tradition, that is, he believed that salvation was a mutual cooperation between God and man; God did 'almost everything', but man had his part to play as well. Erasmus believed and taught that men and women were sinners, but he also taught that sin had not completely disabled them and left them utterly dead towards God. Sin was bad, even very bad, but it was not fatal.

In 1525, Luther responded to Erasmus' 'little book' with what one writer called 'a bomb'. The title of Luther's book says it all: *De servo arbitrio* (*The Bondage of the Will*). Luther thanked Erasmus for raising the issue of man's will: 'You alone ... have attacked the real thing, that is, the essential issue. You have not worried me with those extraneous issues about the Papacy, purgatory, indulgences, and such like — trifles, rather than issues — in respect of which almost all to date have sought my blood ... you, and you alone, have seen the hinge on which all turns, and aimed for the vital spot [literally, 'taken me by the throat']. For that I heartily thank you; for it is more gratifying to me to deal with this issue.'[1]

For Luther, the issue of man's will was not a matter of abstruse theology. The question of the freedom or bondage

---

[1] *The Bondage of the Will: A New Translation of De Servo Arbitrio by J. I Packer and O. R. Johnston* (London: James Clark, 1957), p. 319.

of the will takes us, Luther believed, to the heart of the doctrine of salvation and to the heart of the God-pleasing life. It is significant that Luther calls the issue 'the hinge on which all turns'. Why? For one simple reason: if our wills are not totally in bondage, if there is any residue of essential goodness in any man or woman enabling them to will the good, then salvation is not 'of the Lord'. Salvation becomes a cooperative act, God doing his part and man doing his. For Luther such thinking was both an affront to God and a denial of the gospel, and made the cross 'of none effect'. The Bible could not be any clearer: salvation is wholly the work of God, the result of his grace to us in Christ. Even the faith we believe with is the gift of God (Eph. 2:8). Luther rose to the challenge of responding to Erasmus, not because he was a cross-grained ex-monk, but because he was passionately jealous for the glory of God and the salvation of sinners.

Erasmus thought the issue of free will to be a subject for theologians to discuss and debate and for ordinary Christians to ignore as an idle speculation. For Luther nothing could be further from the truth. Clarity of understanding regarding the limits of the human will was, for him, essential to living a truly Christian life: 'it is not irreligious, idle, or superfluous, but in the highest degree wholesome and necessary, for a Christian to know whether or not his will has anything to do in matters pertaining to salvation'.[1]

[1] *Ibid.*, p. 78.

Luther saw the issue of the will to go to the very heart of the gospel and of the God-pleasing life:

> Now, if I am ignorant of God's works and power, I am ignorant of God himself; and if I do not know God, I cannot worship, praise, give thanks or serve Him, for I do not know how much I should attribute to myself and how much to Him. We need, therefore, to have in mind a clear-cut distinction between God's power and ours, and God's work and ours, if we would live a godly life.[1]

Far from it being recondite and 'superfluous', to know the extent of our will's bondage, or otherwise, could not be more crucial. If we have some virtuous capacity to will and to choose in our sinful natures, then self-confidence and self-righteousness are inescapable concomitants. But if our wills are wholly in bondage to sin and Satan, then salvation must wholly be of God, and the glory completely his. God will have 'no human being' to boast in his presence (1 Cor. 1:29).

Luther's passionate defence of the biblical truth of the bondage of the will was not first motivated by a concern for doctrinal precision, though biblical doctrine is precise. What concerned Luther and motivated him to respond to Erasmus was his concern for God's glory and the salvation of sinners. Where these two concerns animate a theologian, pastor, or a so-called 'ordinary' Christian,

[1] *Ibid.*

man's total inability to will any good whatsoever will be asserted—not casually but passionately—and God's grace in Christ magnified. *Soli Deo Gloria.*

26. Contentment: A Neglected Gospel Grace

Contentment is one of the great Christian graces. Paul tells Timothy that 'there is great gain in godliness with contentment' (1 Tim. 6:6). He tells the church in Philippi 'do not be anxious about anything' (Phil. 4:6). Our Lord Jesus commanded his disciples not to be anxious about their lives (Matt. 6:25). How could Jesus say this? How could he expect and even demand that his disciples not worry? Is this not sheer idealism? Is it not actually absurd to expect believers always to be content and never to be anxious? Clearly not. Our Saviour never engaged in idealism or mere wishful thinking. In fact, Jesus gives his disciples reasons why they should not worry. He makes the observation that worrying never accomplished anything of any significance. But more importantly, Jesus tells his disciples that their lives are cared for, watched over, and dearly loved by their heavenly Father. It is the fatherly love and care of God that is the bedrock of the Christian's contentment.

It is this great truth that Jesus laboured to impress on his disciples as he instructed them on the life of faith in a fallen, hostile world. In Matthew 6, in the midst of his teaching in what is called the Sermon on the Mount, Jesus speaks seven times of 'your Father', three times of 'your heavenly Father', and once of 'our Father'. It is as if Jesus is chiselling into their minds and hearts the truth that the sovereign Lord, 'the great and awesome God' (Dan. 9:4), is their gracious, loving, and generous Father.

Jesus had called these men into a life of consecrated discipleship. He had called them to leave the security of their families and their livelihoods to follow him into a life of evangelical uncertainty. Naturally the Twelve would be asking, 'But how will we eat? Who will care for our bodily needs? What if we need new clothing?' Jesus' response to these legitimate concerns is to set before his disciples the Lord God Almighty's foundational relationship to his children. 'God is your Father, your heavenly Father. He can be trusted to provide for all your needs. You need never be anxious. The Lord God Almighty is bound to you because of your belonging to me.'

Jesus is training his disciples to think theologically, so that they might live contentedly. The theology, or doctrine, of the gospel is not barely propositional. It is, of course, propositional, but gospel truth is for living not merely for confessing. Thus early in the training of the Twelve, Jesus is instructing them in the ABC of the gospel. Nothing is more basic, and more reassuring, in the gospel than learning that in Christ God is our Father. Later in Matthew 7:11, Jesus applies the truth of God's gracious and generous fatherhood to his apprehensive disciples: 'If you then, who are evil, know how to give good gifts to your children, how much more will your Father who is in heaven give good things to those who ask him!' Jesus is encouraging his disciples to think theologically, to reckon on the wonderful truth that God has a father's heart towards his children.

It is this stupendous truth to which Satan seeks to blind us. He magnifies our often adverse circumstances subtly to suggest that God is heartless, indifferent, and even oblivious to our needs. Nothing could be further from the truth. The Father who spared not his only Son for us can be trusted absolutely to act always for our good (see Rom. 8:32).

I doubt there are greater words in the Bible than 'your Father'. Once we were 'children of [his] wrath' (Eph. 2:3) but in Christ we have become his beloved sons and daughters, children he rejoices over with gladness and loud singing (Zeph. 3:17). Be of good cheer. Live in the happy contentment that you have in Christ an always loving, heavenly Father.

27. The Great Commission: Commitment to Gospel Advance

Matthew 28:18-20 are among the best-known, best-loved and most daunting verses in the Bible. They are especially significant because they are the final words of our Lord Jesus Christ prior to his ascension as recorded by Matthew. They have often been described as the church's marching orders, given to it by its risen Lord. The verses are marked by a punctuated refrain of 'theological intentionality': 'All ... all ... all ... all the days [literally] to the end of the age'.

It has been common in the Reformed church to say that the church is defined by three marks: the faithful preaching (and hearing) of God's word, the right administration of the sacraments, and the exercise of godly, gospel-shaped discipline. I have often wondered if a fourth mark should be highlighted: the mark of evangelism. Is it possible for a church truly to be a church of Jesus Christ, the missionary Saviour, if it ignores or is ambivalent to evangelism?

Jesus' public ministry is bookended in Matthew's Gospel by his call to his church to be light and salt in a spiritually dark and decaying world (Matt. 5:13-16), and his call to his church to go into that world and make disciples (Matt. 28:18-20). For the church, mission is not an option to consider but a command to obey. The big question for us is not, *Will we?* but, *How can we best fulfil our calling?*

I should pause here to respond to Christians who believe that the doctrine of predestination and the Great Commission are mutually exclusive. The Bible unambiguously teaches that God predestines all things according to the counsel of his own will and for his own glory (Eph. 1:11). To think that belief in predestination undermines the Great Commission reflects at least three misunderstandings:

First, some people reason that if God has elected certain people, he himself will certainly bring them into his fold, so why evangelise? Because God has not only elected a people to salvation but he has also chosen to use means to fulfil his saving purposes. He has given us a command to obey.

Second, 'If God has only chosen some, we are not in a position to offer Christ to all.' What is assumed here, erroneously, is that in order to have a proper offer you need to have a 'co-extensive provision'. To have a genuine offer you do not need a co-extensive provision: all you need is a situation in which, if somebody complies with the terms of the offer, what has been promised will be provided; that is, if anyone comes to Jesus Christ, God will save them.

Third, 'Calvinists cannot be passionate evangelists.' Nothing could be further from the truth You need but think of George Whitefield and William Carey. It is also forgotten that Calvin's Geneva not only sent out scores of missionaries to France, many of them to certain death, but also initiated a missionary enterprise to Brazil! Far from undermining the urgency of the Great Commission, the truth of sovereign grace motivates us to engage in this commission. It does so in two ways:

First, it assures us that our witness to Christ will be effective, not in terms of our own persuasiveness but in terms of the sovereign action of God (Isa. 55:10-11).

Second, if you do not believe in sovereign grace, all you can do is to offer a tentative salvation: 'God has done so much, now you must do your part to be saved.' If you believe in sovereign grace you will say, 'God has done it all; come and receive what you could never deserve.'

It seems clear from the structure of these verses that the commission Jesus gave to his disciples is a covenantally-shaped commission. The fundamental features of an ancient covenant are found in Jesus' words: first a pre-amble, then a stipulation, and then a promise.

First, there is a preamble which takes the form of a 'great claim' (verse 18). In giving his disciples this great commission, Jesus is first claiming the right to do so. 'All authority in heaven and on earth has been given to me.' Jesus is speaking here of an authority that was not native to him as the Son of God, but that had been given to him as the Mediator who would soon accomplish the work entrusted to him by his Father (Phil. 2:9-11). It is the Lord and Mediator of the cosmos who stands before this little band of disciples to commission them.

Second, there is a stipulation which takes the form of a 'great commission' (verses 19-20a). You don't need much imagination to picture the scene: a band of eleven recently rehabilitated failures, given the commission to 'Go and make disciples of all nations.' It would be laughable were it not for the '*therefore*'! It is because Jesus has all power in heaven and on earth, and because he will himself be with them always, that he can give these men such a commission (see 2 Cor. 4:7).

There are a number of features to notice in the commission:

1. It was a deeply *daunting* commission. They were to go and make disciples of 'all nations'. How daunting was that! But the daunting universal character of their mission is compounded by the character of the men commissioned by Jesus to be his ambassadors. They had all deserted him. Peter had denied him. But God delights to take the weak things of the world to confound the strong (1 Cor. 1:27).

2. It was a manifestly *ecclesial* commission. Converts were to be baptised 'in the name [singular!] of the Father and of the Son and of the Holy Spirit'. Baptism belongs to the heart of the gospel (Acts 2:38-39, 41-42). In the structure of the sentence, baptising and teaching are both subordinate to 'make disciples'. In other words, a person becomes a disciple by being baptised and by being taught. Disciples are baptised, instructed believers, not simply people who have made a 'decision' for Jesus. In the New Testament, baptism was the public rite that initiated a believer into the fellowship, worship, and service of the church. The great crowd of converts at Pentecost 'devoted

themselves to … the fellowship' (Acts 2:42). Belonging to the visible church, sharing in its worship and witness, living under its care and oversight, was the privilege of every new convert. Christianity is not an agglomeration of saved individuals; it is a community, a family, a body, a temple of saved sinners. We are saved to belong.

3. It was a self-conscious *trinitarian* commission. The great and glorious truth of God's triune being lies at the heart of biblical Christianity. I wonder if Christians sufficiently take the time to ponder the wonder that is the triune God, and the wonder that is our trinitarian salvation.

4. It was a greatly *privileged* commission. They were to teach converts to observe 'all that I have commanded you'. Seeing sinners saved is but the beginning of the church's mission in the world. Converts are to be taught 'the truth as it is in Jesus', that they might 'grow in the grace and knowledge of our Lord and Saviour Jesus Christ' (2 Pet. 3:18).

Third, there is a promise which takes the form of a 'great comfort' (verse 20b). Jesus could hardly have concluded his daunting commission with more comforting and encouraging words: 'And behold, I am with you always, to the end of the age'! I love the 'Beholds' of the Bible. A more literal translation of Matthew's Greek would be, 'all the days to the end of the age': the bad days as well as the good days, the hard as well as the easy, the sorrowful as well as the joyful. Jesus knew that these men, the foundation stones of his church (Eph. 2:20), were weak and poor, at their best mere 'jars of clay'. So he leaves them, not with the weight of the task, but with the assured comfort of his presence. The one who is with the church is the one to whom all authority in heaven and earth has been given.

Up till now all of Matthew's narrative sections have been followed by long discourses. But his final narrative (chapters 26-28) has no concluding discourse. Why? Because *we* are to provide the final discourse! Jesus does not spell out 'how' his church is to 'go and make disciples', except that we are to do so with the assurance of his cosmic-dominating presence with us.

J. I. Packer wrote that, 'Evangelism is a Christian being a Christian.' He was making the vastly important point that evangelism is not first 'things we do', but a lifestyle that proclaims Jesus Christ is Lord. Would that many people would look at the way Christians live, and think, and even say, 'Twinkle, twinkle, little star, *how I wonder what you are!*'

28. Not Losing Heart:
Cultivating Gospel & Ministerial Perseverance

The temptation to lose heart in the Christian life and in the gospel ministry is a temptation that you will battle with till your dying breath. The reason for this is so obvious that I hardly need to mention it, but I will. We cannot climb out of our own skin. We are what we are—'frail children of dust and feeble as frail'—and that is why temptation has a natural landing-ground within us. We know that sin's guilt and prevailing power have been removed, but we know only too well that we have not yet been delivered from sin's remaining, troubling presence.

In 2 Corinthians 4:7, Paul likens gospel ministers to 'jars of clay', ordinary, easily broken, nondescript. When we take stock and look at ourselves, we can hardly get over how shallow we are, how inconsistent, how lacking we are in love and zeal for our Saviour. Is there a day when you do not cry out to the Lord with John Wesley, 'Cure me, Lord, of my intermittent piety'? And if we add to our deep sense of personal unfitness for gospel ministry the lack of saving and sanctifying fruit from our ministerial endeavours, then the temptation to lose heart can be almost overwhelming.

Paul was no stranger to the temptation to lose heart. For example, he writes, 'For we were so utterly burdened beyond our strength that we despaired of life itself. Indeed, we felt that we had received the sentence of death' (2 Cor. 1:8-9). In 2 Corinthians 4:8ff. he speaks of being afflicted in every way, persecuted, struck down, always carrying in the body the death of Jesus. Who is sufficient for these things? Certainly not you and certainly not I.

In the previous chapter Paul wrote: 'Such is the confidence that we have through Christ toward God. Not that we are sufficient in ourselves to claim anything as coming from us, but our sufficiency is from God, who has made us competent to be ministers of a new covenant, not of the letter but of the Spirit. For the letter kills, but the Spirit gives life' (2 Cor. 3:4-6). Paul understood that his 'sufficiency' as a gospel minister lay wholly in God. That is true for all Christians and not just for preachers. But how does God mediate his 'sufficiency' to his servants? What was it that kept the apostle from losing heart as he served the Lord?

First, the splendour of the ministry God had given him. This is the ministry he has been speaking about throughout the previous chapter (cf. 3:6). It is a ministry that 'gives life'. He takes us to the glorious heart of this new covenant ministry in 4:5-6. This is the astonishing privilege given by God to every gospel minister. He did not give this ministry to angels but to men like us, 'jars of clay', fragile, easily knocked, mere lumps of dust. Samuel Rutherford—saintly, Christ-saturated Samuel Rutherford—wrote, 'One thing qualifies me for Christ, my abominable vileness.' Your abominable vileness does not disqualify you from the gospel ministry. When a jeweller wants to display a brilliant diamond, he sets it against a background that will show off the beauty and brilliance of the gem. As Christ's ambassadors proclaim the grace and glory of the gospel of God, we do so out of lives that are mere jars of clay. God engineers it this way to show that the excellency and power is of him and not of us (2 Cor. 4:7b). God does not need to use any means to accomplish his saving purposes, but he chooses ordinarily to do so. He even calls his servants his 'fellow workers' (1 Cor. 3:9).

One of my fears, a fear that almost haunts me, is the fear that in my life I will lose the sense of the sheer wonder of the gospel and end up simply iterating truths. Robert Dabney speaks about this in his book *Sacred Rhetoric:*[1]

> Without a sacred weight of character, the most splendid rhetoric will win only short-lived applause; with it, the plainest scriptural instructions are eloquent to win souls. Eloquence may dazzle and please, holiness of life convinces.

Second, the wonder of the mercy God had bestowed on him. This new covenant ministry which proclaims Jesus Christ as Lord was given to Paul 'by the mercy of God' (2 Cor. 4:1). How did Paul end up a gospel minister? How does any man end up a gospel minister? How does anyone end up a Christian? *By the mercy of God*. It was not your gifts that qualified you to be a gospel minister. Yes, there are necessary gifts, the gift of preaching, the gift of pastoring among others. But the root reason, the radical reason, why anyone is a gospel minister is the mercy of God. Mercy is sheer undeserved kindness. Paul could never get over the sense of wonder that to him, the chief of sinners, God had mercifully entrusted the proclamation of 'the unsearchable riches of Christ' (Eph. 3:7-9). Paul writes

---

[1] Reprinted by the Trust under the title *Evangelical Eloquence*.

here of being the 'least' of all God's people. Actually, the Greek is starker and more ungrammatical. Paul writes, not 'least', but 'leaster'. He uses the comparative and not the superlative. Why? Because, I think, he is so overwhelmed by the grace given to him that a sense of wonder transcends the rules of grammar in his experience. Can you in any way identify with Paul's experience?

It is an astonishing thing that the Lord who is able to do all he pleases, using no means whatsoever, has nevertheless chosen to use mere men to be his gospel ambassadors. Our calling is to ensure we are the purest means, the cleanest instruments for the Lord to use in the work of the gospel. And what is true for gospel ministers holds true for every Christian.

Do you, do I, remotely possess a 'sacred weight of character'? Are we men and women who can never get over the amazing fact that to us—yes, to us—God has entrusted the work of preaching the gospel and bearing witness to his Son?

These two *desiderata* matter as much as, even more than, theological competence. Ultimately, effective preaching and effective witnessing are the overflow of a life. What overflows from your life to the people you preach and witness to?

29. *Being a Witness: Sharing the Gospel*

If someone—a neighbour, a fellow worker, or fellow scholar—were to ask you, 'What exactly is the gospel?', what would you say? Perhaps I could ask you to stop reading, pick up a pen, and write in a few brief sentences what is the essence of the gospel. It would be a good exercise—and perhaps a sobering and salutary one—to crystallise your thoughts regarding the gospel.

So, where did you begin? Where should anyone begin? I suppose it depends on who asked you the question. Did they have a 'Christian' background? Were they nominal or militant atheists? Were they Muslims, or Hindus? Were they Dawkinsian secularists? I would guess that what you say would, in measure, depend on where your questioner was coming from.

One danger, however, is that you become intimidated by your questioner: 'I don't know much if anything about Islam, Hinduism, atheism, secularism. I have no training in apologetics (defending the faith). My understanding of "presuppositional philosophy" is nil.' But do you have to be trained and well-read to be an effective witness to your Saviour? Certainly, it can be hugely helpful to read good books and listen to insightful teachers. We are called to give a 'reason' for the hope that is in us. But effective

Christian witness is not dependent on having theological and philosophical training!

Our Lord Jesus said on one significant occasion to his disciples, 'You are the light of the world. A city set on a hill cannot be hidden … let your light shine before others, so that they may see your good works and give glory to your Father who is in heaven' (Matt. 5:14-16). At the heart of effective Christian witness is a godly, Christ-honouring, 'do-gooding' life. What God is most pleased to use for his glory and the extension of his kingdom is not a well-stocked mind but a Christlike life (the two, of course, are not mutually exclusive). What the Holy Spirit blesses is not well-constructed arguments and deep learning, but humble-hearted, prayerful dependence on him who alone can unstop deaf ears and illumine sin-darkened minds. Again let me say that an educated mind and a Spirit-dependent heart are not mutually exclusive: far from it. But too easily we are guilty of de-spiritualising gospel witness. What I mean is that we underplay the mighty, sovereign, sin-vanquishing power of God the Holy Spirit as we open our mouths to testify to our Saviour. Too often we are more conscious of our own inadequacies than of the grace and power of the one for whom nothing is impossible.

We had an evangelistic book-table ministry in the church I served in Cambridge. Every Saturday we would spend time in the Market Square giving out literature and engaging passers-by in conversation. All who helped in any way would be the first to say, 'Oh that I had a better mind and deeper understanding!' But our great 'book-table need' was prayerful, humble dependence on God the Holy Spirit.

That is your great need as you seek to answer the question, 'What is the gospel?' Your words may be few and stammering; but it is 'not by might, nor by power, but by my Spirit, says the LORD of hosts' (Zech. 4:6).

So who knows what God might be pleased to do with a few simple words of testimony, backed up by a life in which Jesus Christ reigns in grace? When someone asked John Knox to account for the remarkable success of the Scottish Reformation, he replied, 'God gave his Holy Spirit to simple men in great abundance.'

30. 'My Father Is Always Working': Gospel Confidence

It is only too easy for Christians to become daunted and deeply pessimistic. The world we live in is a dark, and, presently, an ever-darkening, place. The gospel of our Lord Jesus Christ is increasingly and publicly mocked and marginalised throughout society, particularly in the media. Our government passes legislation that defies the living God. Our churches, most of them, are small and struggling. Evangelical Christianity is awash with theological and moral compromise. You might well be forgiven for thinking, Is it any wonder believers are daunted and deeply pessimistic?

Do we have any reason, however, for being downbeat and discouraged? Allow me to remind you of our Lord's words in John 5:17: 'My Father is always working.'[1] *Always!* Not occasionally. Not much of the time. But all of the time. Our God is never indolent, never merely watching the world's progress from the sidelines. He is always at work; and if he is always at work, how can we ever be daunted and discouraged? I know that some who read this chapter will be going through sore trials. Others will have legacies of deep disappointments. Some will be in churches where little if any apparent progress has been seen for years. And yet, 'My Father is always working.'

It is true that our God's working is not always, or even often, obvious.

> He hides himself so wondrously,
>   As if there were no God:
> He is least seen when all the powers
>   Of ill are most abroad.[2]

Nonetheless, he is always at work, fulfilling his sure, sovereign, blessed purposes. He is never idle. His working is never frantic or uncertain, but always calm, deliberate and perfectly purposeful: 'Our God is in the heavens; he does all that he pleases' (Psa. 115:3).

---

[1] My own translation.
[2] From F. W. Faber's hymn 'Oh, It Is Hard to Work for God'.

If nothing else, this great truth should inspire at least two things in our lives: First, we should never lose heart. Our God is working and nothing and no one can stand against him. History, with all its dark uncertainties and apparently uncontrolled wickedness, is overseen and punctuated by the Sovereign God who works. This is not an excuse for us to sit back and smirk at our circumstances. But it is a wonderful encouragement for Christians not to lose heart, not to become daunted and disappointed. God is at work, *always*.

Second, we are encouraged to live by faith and not by sight. What is faith? At heart it is trusting God for who he is and believing his word, whatever it says. Faith says, 'I believe God.' So, when we read, 'My Father is always working', however downbeat and seemingly bleak our circumstances, we believe God's word.

I have little doubt that it often pleases the Lord to withhold the obvious evidences of his working in order to teach us the grace of faith. This truth is put starkly and remarkably in Isaiah 50:10: 'Let him who walks in darkness and has no light trust in the name of the LORD and rely on his God.' But faith is more than trusting reposefully in God; it is believing that God is able to accomplish whatsoever he pleases.

Because our God is an ever-working God, whose power is limitless and unconquerable, there is no saying what he may well be pleased to accomplish. 'You do not have, because you do not ask' (James 4:2)! God's sovereign working is not an excuse for us to sit back and drift with whatever tide comes our way. No, a thousand times no! Does the Lord himself not tell us that his Father in heaven will give the Holy Spirit to those who ask him? (Luke 11:13). Faith lays hold of the God who always works. It pleads his promises, that his Son may be glorified and his people saved.

'My Father is always working.' Are these not wonderfully encouraging words? Do they not pierce our gloom and despondency? The Lord will not lose one of his own. He will present his church to himself as a spotless, perfect bride. Take heart! The God who is for us in Christ, and who rules the heavens and the earth, is always working.

31. *The Sweetness of God: The Gospel's Marrow*

The Confessions of St Augustine is a great and compelling read, a 300-page prayer that illuminates Augustine's search for God and for life. As I read the opening chapters I was struck by a word that Augustine regularly uses and that had not registered with me before. Again and again as he speaks to God Augustine refers to him as his 'sweetness' (or 'delight'). I began to note every time this word is used, and other similar affectional terms. While he also speaks of God's majesty and sovereignty and power, it was his use of the word 'sweetness' that captured and captivated my attention.

The thing that had made such a great impact on Augustine when he came to a living, saving faith in Jesus Christ was God's tender and kind dealings with him throughout the years of his spiritual quest. Now a believer in Christ, Augustine had tasted that 'the LORD is good' (Psa. 34:8), and discovered that this goodness was 'sweet'.

'My sweetness.' As I thought about this striking statement I began to ask myself whether I also could call the Lord 'my sweetness'?

It was Jonathan Edwards, the great eighteenth-century New England pastor-theologian, who wrote, 'True religion, in great part, consists in holy affections'. Edwards maintained that the Christian faith is natively affectional. The gospel does not come only to transform our minds and reform our lives; it comes to implant within us godly affections. First among all truly Christian affections is heartfelt love to God, Father, Son and Holy Spirit. In the gospel God reveals himself to us supremely as a God of love and grace. It was because the Father 'so loved the world' that he gave his one and only Son. It was because the Lord Jesus Christ loved us that he gave himself for us (Gal. 2:20). It is his love for us that draws out love to him.

God's love to us is eternal, unchanging, and altogether undeserved. He could justly and righteously have damned us, but he chose in unfathomable grace to love us in Christ.

Yes, the Lord is of purer eyes than even to look on sin. He is almighty, transcendent, majestic in holiness. But in his love to sinners he is truly 'sweet', inexpressibly sweet.

John Owen makes the telling observation in his remarkable work *On Communion with God* that many Christians think there is no sweetness in God towards sinners except what was purchased by the high price of Jesus' blood. For Owen this is nothing short of blasphemy and turns the gospel on its head. The gospel is not, Because Jesus died for us God now loves us; but rather: Because God loved us Jesus died for us! There is sweetness in God towards sinners that predates the cross, a sweetness that brought him to send forth his Son to be the propitiation for our sins, and not for our sins only, but for the sins of the whole world (1 John 2:2).

It is when we begin to sense the embrace of our heavenly Father's love for us in Christ that we begin to understand why Augustine could call the Lord his 'sweetness'.

'My sweetness.' Are these not moving and deeply searching words? They are to me and, I trust, they will be to you.

32. The Faithful God:
The Gospel's Firm Foundation

One of the most deeply moving, and constantly recurring, features in the Bible is God's unyielding commitment to his covenant people. It is altogether breathtaking to see God's enduring faithfulness to a people who were in turns rebellious, disobedient, forgetful and plain ungrateful towards him. This unyielding faithfulness is graphically illustrated in the Israelites' confession of sin in Nehemiah 9. As they survey their spiritually checkered history, and especially their wilful defections from their covenant Lord, the people plead the enduring faithfulness and grace of his character: 'But you are a forgiving God, gracious and compassionate, slow to anger and abounding in love. Therefore you did not desert them, even when they cast for themselves an image of a calf and said, "This is your god, who brought you up out of Egypt," or when they committed awful blasphemies' (verses 17-18 NIV). These are astonishing words. Of course, as Paul discovered, such unfettered grace can be used as an excuse for living antinomian lives (read Rom. 6:1ff.). To the child of God, however, the grace of God's character, far from being an excuse to go on sinning, is the greatest incentive to hate sin, and with the Spirit's help to put sin to death in our lives.

It is true, however, that God reveals the grace of his character not merely for our admiration, but also for our emulation. What Paul writes to Christians in Ephesus brings us face to face with the life believers are called to in our union with Jesus Christ: 'Be kind and compassionate to one another, forgiving each other, just as in Christ God forgave you. Be imitators of God, therefore, as dearly loved children …' (Eph. 4:32–5:1 NIV). We are to treat one another with the same patience, forbearance, generosity, and kindness as the Lord has treated us. We are to mirror and reflect in our lives something of the 'family likeness'. This is daunting, to say the least. And yet this is the life to which every Christian is called.

This high and holy calling to be imitators of God in the way we treat one another (face to face and when speaking with others!) is pressed upon the Ephesian Christians by Paul (read Eph. 4:1-2). What is so important for us to grasp is the reason why Paul so passionately urges Christians to 'bear with one another in love'; do so, he says, to 'maintain the unity of the Spirit in the bond of peace'. Christian unity was not a marginal doctrine for Paul. Nor was it something that was of peripheral concern to him. Christian unity, for Paul, was of paramount importance. It was his concern to guard Christian unity, the unity that all believers have through our union with Jesus Christ, that prompted Paul to urge God's people to 'be completely humble and gentle [and] be patient, bearing with one another in love' (Eph. 4:2 NIV). As he lies chained in a Roman prison, the apostle's heart pleads for God's own people to cherish their unity in Christ and to do all they can to preserve and beautify that Spirit-wrought unity.

Never has the church more needed to hear and heed these words. We live in a world obsessed with its own rights. The 'pick and mix' character of consumerism has invaded the life of the church, and all but absolutised the 'rights' and desires of individual believers to pursue their own concerns with little regard for other Christians. The slogans of society's gurus are increasingly heard within professing Bible-believing churches: 'Be true to yourself!' 'Find your own space!' 'Develop a positive self-image!' 'Recover self-esteem!' It is little wonder, if Christians are listening to society's self-image gurus, that the evangelical church is so fragmented, self-absorbed, and increasingly a stranger to the objective, abidingly true, and life-enriching doctrines of Holy Scripture. Didn't our Lord Jesus Christ tell us that we would find our life only if we lost it; that only if we denied ourselves and took up our cross could we follow him? (read Mark 8:34-35).

Self-absorption lies at the root of much that scars the life and witness of our Saviour's church today. Forgetting ourselves and seeking the good of others is not only healthy, it is a spiritual grace that helps to 'maintain the unity of the Spirit in the bond of peace'.

So let me conclude with three watchwords that a good friend regularly would say to me: 'Ian, is what you intend to say *true, kind, necessary*?' Guarding the unity of the

Spirit for Christ's sake is the duty to which every Christian is called. So, says Paul, 'Let all bitterness and wrath and anger and clamour and slander be put away from you, along with all malice [note he is writing such words to Christians!]. Be kind to one another, tenderhearted, forgiving one another, as God in Christ forgave you. Therefore be imitators of God, as beloved children.'

33. The Covenant of Redemption: The Gospel's Eternal Roots

Every phase of our Saviour's life was shaped and styled by his self-conscious sense that he had come from heaven to do not his own will but the will of him who sent him (John 6:38). Indeed, it would not be over-stretching the point to say that John 6:37-40 is programmatic of the whole course of Jesus' life of covenant obedience to his Father. There he stands before us not as a private individual but as the appointed covenant head of God's elect. It is as the one appointed by God to be his servant and his people's head that Jesus declares his self-denying obedience to the will of his Father, to the end that he should lose not one of those given to him by his Father (John 6:39). This truth alone makes sense of everything our Lord did throughout the course of his earthly life and continues to do throughout the course of his present heavenly life as the God-Man. All he does is for all those he represents (Rom. 5:18-19; 1 Cor. 15:22). This truth is imbedded in our Lord's self-conscious sense of having been 'given' a people to save by his Father.

This holy resolve to obey his Father, whatever the cost (and it cost him everything), did not, however, begin and develop primarily within the psychology of his sinless humanity. In the councils of eternity, the Son of God, with his Father and the Spirit, conspired and decreed in astonishing love to create a world, and out of the sinful mass of that world, all fallen in its appointed covenant head Adam, to redeem a people, for their own glory. This *pactum salutis* lies at the heart of the biblical plan of salvation and shaped the earthly, and the present heavenly, life of our Saviour. Although excellent men like Thomas Boston and John Dick would not accept the idea of a separate covenant of redemption, most Reformed divines have seen the wisdom of distinguishing between the covenant of grace and the covenant of redemption. John Owen, for one, argued for a covenant of redemption, made with Christ for the benefit of the elect. The effect of this covenant was that Christ, by fulfilling the terms of the covenant, secured all the blessings that flow to believing sinners from the covenant of grace. Owen highlighted three conditions of this covenant):[1] First, Christ is to assume human nature and be

[1] See Sinclair B. Ferguson, *John Owen on the Christian Life* (Edinburgh: Banner of Truth Trust, 1987), p. 26.

made flesh. Second, he is to be the servant of his Father in giving obedience to his law as the appointed mediator of his people. Third, he is to make atonement for sin and in doing so bear on behalf of God's elect his just judgment with respect to the broken covenant of works. All this Jesus did as the second Adam and last man, in our nature.

One point I would add: It has always seemed strange to me that the Holy Spirit operates at best peripherally and at worst anonymously in many explications of the covenant of redemption. It may be that the Father and the Son are more apparently prominent in those passages where this covenant relationship is highlighted. It must, however, be asserted that the Holy Spirit, no less than the Father and the Son, is active in the arrangements of the covenant of redemption. This is clear, not only from the application of the *opera ad extra trinitatis indivisa sunt* (the external works of the Trinity cannot be divided) principle, but no less from the essential role of the Holy Spirit in 'covenanting' to uphold and enable the Son in his obedient fulfilling of the requirements of the covenant of redemption (Isa. 42:1; 11:2).

This sense of living under the constraints of the 'council of redemption' profoundly shaped the whole course of our Saviour's earthly mission. His covenant engagement was not a piece of theoretical theology; it was a dynamic that moulded the whole course of Jesus' life.

1. *It measured the pace of his mission.* The whole course of his earthly mission was directed by a divinely

devised timetable. The marked self-consciousness of living in obedient servanthood to his Father reveals itself in a significant way throughout John's Gospel. Again and again we find our Lord shaping his earthly agenda not by the circumstances of the moment, but by the realisation that the dominating, controlling motif in his life was a 'decreed hour'. At the wedding in Cana, he tells his mother who is expecting him to remedy, in some way, the lack of wine, 'My hour has not yet come' (John 2:4). Later as the shadow of the cross begins to penetrate his soul, he declares, 'Now is my soul troubled, And what shall I say? "Father, save me from this hour"? But for this purpose I have come to this hour. Father, glorify your name!' (John 12:27-28a). This led to our Lord at times strategically withdrawing from confrontation with his enemies. He was never motivated by cowardice, but always by a submissive obedience to the decreed timetable of his Father. Every step of the way our Lord knew that his times were in his Father's hands. This truth ought no less to measure the pace of the believer's life. Our times are also in his hands. Even with our different temperaments and personalities, should not our lives betray that truth? The predestinarian character of biblical religion ought, above all else, to give our lives a sense of poise and unruffled assurance, even when all around us others are losing their heads.

2. *It moulded the character of his mission.* Our Lord had come to be God's 'obedient Servant' and he avoided no necessary cost in fulfilling the willingly received commission

given to him by his Father. As the perfect image of the Father (John 14:9), our Lord can be seen insisting on the costly career of inflexible obedience to his Father's word. Nowhere is this more movingly described for us than in his agony in the garden and in its immediate aftermath. Mark tells us, he 'began to be greatly distressed and troubled'. He told Peter, James and John, 'My soul is overwhelmed with sorrow to the point of death' (Mark 14:33-34 NIV). And yet he embraces the cup his Father had prepared for him, the cup he had committed himself to drinking when the triune God devised the covenant of redemption. The terms of the covenant constrained our beloved Saviour to walk the way of inflexible, but ever willingly given, obedience. Never imagine that it was effortless for our Lord Jesus to walk that way. Obedience to his Father cost him everything! For him there was no other way to live. He was living out the obedience he had promised to give to his Father in time eternal. Faithfulness to his Father required it; the salvation of the elect of God depended on it. The Saviour's servanthood was therefore a covenantal servanthood. Nothing less would secure God's decreed salvation for all his people.

3. *It motivated the spirit of his earthly mission*. He had come from the Father as his Servant. He delighted to offer to the Father the covenant obedience he pledged himself to in the eternal council — 'I delight to do your will, O my God' (Psa. 40:8). The fact that he was acting in obedience to his Father's will in fulfilling all the conditions of

the covenant of redemption drew from our Lord Jesus the motivating spirit that rendered his obedience pleasing to his Father. There was nothing forced or grudging or reluctant about Jesus' obedience. So much so that the Father split the heavens to say, 'You are my beloved Son; with you I am well pleased' (Mark 1:11). In our Lord Jesus' life we see the pre-eminent value of 'heart' obedience. We can never be reminded too often that our God looks on the heart. It is only too easy for us, with all our Reformed theology, to drift into mindless, mechanical, clinical servanthood. As the Father's Servant-King, our Saviour lived *coram deo* (before the face of God). This is the essence of biblical piety. This is why we read again and again throughout the Old Testament that the most meticulous performance of God-ordained ritual cannot begin to compensate for the absence of heart worship and love: 'The sacrifices of God are a broken spirit; a broken and contrite heart, O God, you will not despise' (Psa. 51:17; cf. Isa. 1:10ff.).

4. *It inspired the unruffled confidence that impregnated his earthly mission* (cf. John 6:37, 39-40). Our Servant-King never wavered in the execution of his office, as was prophesied of him in Isaiah 42:3. Never was our Lord for one moment uncertain about the outcome of his mission. This assurance meant that the whole course of his earthly life was marked by a sure, unruffled sense of what he was about and where he was going. He knew that his Father's promise to support and strengthen him by the indwelling

presence and ministry of the Holy Spirit would absolutely be fulfilled. When he exhorted his disciples to be anxious about nothing because 'your heavenly Father knows', he was simply saying to them what the heavenly Father had said (as it were) to him. This is something we all need to learn. Graceful, well-balanced Christian living is not the fruit of a particular kind of temperament, but the fruit of knowing that our times are in our gracious and sovereign Lord's hands. 'The Lord is my helper; I will not fear; what can man do to me?' (Heb. 13:6). Practical, godly living is imbedded in deeply understood theology. The doctrine of God, understanding who God is and his covenanted commitment to his people, breathes poise and quiet, unruffled confidence into the Christian's heart. So it did to our Lord Jesus, the proto-typical man of faith.

5. *It manifested the loving, merciful attitude of God that was the animating heartbeat of his earthly mission.* What prompted God to send his only Son to be the Saviour of the world? In a word, 'love'. 'God so loved the world that he gave his only Son' (John 3:16); 'God shows his love for us in that while we were still sinners, Christ died for us' (Rom. 5:8). Sovereign love to rebellious, judgment-deserving sinners was the fountain out of which redemption flowed to a lost world. It was not surprising, then, that this love was the heartbeat that animated every step of Jesus' mission. 'When he saw the crowds', Matthew tells us, 'he had compassion for them, because they were harassed and helpless, like sheep without a shepherd' (Matt. 9:36).

When the 'rich young ruler' came to him asking, 'What must I do to inherit eternal life?', 'Jesus, looking at him, loved him' (Mark 10:21). When the Pharisees expressed their disgust that he should receive sinners and eat with them, Jesus told them a series of parables culminating in the parable of the prodigal son (Luke 15:11-32). In this parable, Jesus likened God to the father of the lost son who, when he saw his repentant son heading for home, 'was filled with compassion ... threw his arms around him and kissed him' (verse 20 NIV). The Pharisees could not understand Jesus because they did not understand that 'God is love'. Jesus' disregard for social and traditional religious conventions was due to his compassion for sinners—love for sinners made him seek, by all means, to save some. The compassion that shone through Jesus' earthly life was the overflow of the covenant of redemption. It was this love, expressed in obedience to the will of his Father, that kept Jesus on track and led him to embrace the dark, unspeakable desolation of the cross. It was our sins that held him there, but only because love was offering itself, the just for the unjust, to bring us to God.

It is a wonderful thing that the triune God should have resolved in sovereign, unfathomable grace to love a world of lost sinners and save them. He bound himself to do so and fulfilled that 'binding' when the Lord Jesus Christ made propitiation for our sins and rose in triumph over sin and death and hell. It is little wonder Paul exclaimed, 'Oh, the depth of the riches and wisdom and knowledge of

God! ... For from him and through him and to him are all things. To him be glory for ever. Amen' (Rom. 11:33, 36).

34. The Grace of Election:
What Gospel Life Looks Like

It is often missed that the doctrine of God's sovereign election of sinners to life is presented in the Bible not as a puzzle to solve, far less a truth to make us proud, but as a truth to humble us and then inspire us to live lives to God's praise and glory. This is not something that many people outside or even inside the church grasp. The doctrine of election is thought to breed pride and a careless attitude to godly living. If I am an elect sinner (so the thinking goes) then I must be better than the rest, and it doesn't matter how I live because I am one of God's 'chosen ones'. This thinking is so very far removed from the thinking and teaching of God's word.

In Colossians 3:12ff., Paul exhorts God's 'holy and beloved' people to clothe themselves with 'compassion, kindness, humility, meekness, and patience'. He goes on to encourage them to 'Bear with each other and forgive whatever grievances [they] may have against one another', just as the Lord had forgiven them (verse 13 NIV). What is striking to notice is the truth that Paul sets before them as the foundation for his exhortation to godliness: 'Put on then, *as God's chosen ones*, holy and beloved, compassion, kindness, humility ...' (verse 12).

Paul is following here the invariable grammar of Holy Scripture; that is, he is grounding exhortation in gracious doctrine. We see this principial pattern in Exodus 20:2-3.

First, the Lord reminds his people that he is the God who brought them out of the land of bondage (verse 2), who carried them on eagles' wings and brought them to himself (Exod. 19:4). It is only then that he commands them, 'You shall have no other gods before me.' God graciously provides his people with a powerful incentive to obedience. He chooses not to constrain obedience by divine fiat only. Rather, he resolves to 'woo' them to a life of believing obedience by reminding them of his great grace towards them. Failure to appreciate the gracious context of the giving of the law has led, throughout the centuries, to a practical dislocation of law from grace. This has resulted in 'legal obedience', which is the religion of devils, not the religion of the God of grace.

It is this same pattern and principle that we see operating in Colossians 3:12ff. Paul begins by reminding the Colossians who they are: 'God's chosen ones', his elect people. They have been the recipients of God's sovereign, distinguishing love. They did not first choose him; he chose them. But for God's distinguishing, electing love, they would yet be 'children of wrath, like the rest of mankind' (Eph. 2:3). But sovereign, electing love intervened and rescued them from their hell-bound state. For Paul this is presented to his readers as a wonderful incentive to godly, Christlike living. Godliness of life is the response of love to love, of forgiven love to forgiving love.

Too often sanctification, likeness to Christ, is divorced from God's electing love and becomes in the process a duty more than a desire. Of course, sanctification is our Christian duty; but it is a duty of love, not a duty of mere demand. The same principle operates in human relationships. A wife is under divine obligation to submit to her husband (Eph. 5:22). But how is that submission to be drawn out from her? Yes, it is a divine command she is to obey, whether she feels like obeying it or not. But in the theological grammar of the Scriptures, what follows in Ephesians 5:25ff. is surely to be connected to verse 22. Husbands are to 'love [their] wives, as Christ loved the church and gave himself up for her'. So, as husbands self-denyingly love their wives, cherishing them to the point of laying down their lives for them, wives have gospel submission sweetly drawn from them. Love responds to love.

This is Paul's unvarying pastoral methodology. You see the point more panoramically in Romans 12:1ff. For eleven chapters Paul has been expounding the astonishing grace of God in Christ. As he concludes his exposition of this grace his heart and mind overflow in soaring doxology (11:33-36). It is at this critical point that Paul summons the Romans to 'present [their] bodies as a living sacrifice, holy and acceptable to God' (12:1). The call to sanctification is rooted and grounded in the prior 'mercies of God' (12:1a).

Election is not conceived for one moment as a deterrent to sanctification; in fact the exact opposite is true. For Paul, the one inevitable response of a forgiven sinner to the wonder and mystery of God's sovereign election is undivided surrender and whole-hearted commitment. The response of a believing sinner to God's sovereign, electing love is well expressed in Robert Murray M'Cheyne's hymn:

> Chosen, not for good in me,
>   Wakened up from wrath to flee;
> Hidden in the Saviour's side,
>   By the Spirit sanctified;
> Teach me, Lord, on earth to show,
>   By my love, how much I owe.

Where this song of adoring wonder at God's electing love is absent from our lives, it is hardly possible that this love has penetrated and captured our hearts and our wills. This is why the New Testament is adamant that nothing less than a transformed life is the evidence of truly experienced electing love. Paul tells the Ephesians, 'we are his workmanship, created in Christ Jesus for good works, which God prepared beforehand, that we should walk in them' (Eph. 2:10). He tells the Thessalonians, 'We know, brothers loved by God, that he has chosen you, because our gospel came to you not only in word, but also in power and in the Holy Spirit and with full conviction' (1 Thess. 1:4-5). In the previous verse, Paul highlights the fruit this produced in their lives: 'your work of faith and labour of love and steadfastness of hope in our Lord Jesus Christ'.

In similar vein, Peter tells the exiles of the Dispersion we have been chosen 'according to the foreknowledge of God the Father, in the sanctification of the Spirit, for obedience to Jesus Christ and for sprinkling with his blood' (1 Pet. 1:2). Where life-transformation is absent, electing love is not present. Election inevitably produces a morally transformed lifestyle, because election is 'in Christ' (Eph. 1:4) and makes us, through faith, partakers of the life of Christ.

This is why gospel imperatives to godliness are never bare commands, but commands that highlight and are rooted in our new identity as men and women who have died with Christ and been raised with Christ to live a new life (Rom. 6:1-14).

The doctrine of election is not part of Calvinism's quirkiness; it belongs to the warp and woof of God's self-disclosure in the Bible. It is a wonderful assurance to the Christian believer that, come what may, our salvation rests secure because it is anchored in God's invincible, electing grace.

In his book *The Old Evangelicalism* Iain H. Murray reminds us that, 'It was no accident that in the sixteenth century the experience of assurance revived simultaneously with the recovery of the truths called Calvinism.' Murray goes on to quote Calvin:

> We may rejoice in this, that God will have pity upon us until the end, and that he will keep us: and although he suffer us to stumble, yea so as to fall, we shall be recovered and upholden by his hand.

And how is it that we can trust in this? Without election it is impossible: but when we know that the Father has committed us unto the keeping of his Son, we are certain that we shall be maintained by him unto the end.

Is election, then, a doctrine to make man proud and arrogant? God forbid! It stirs forgiven sinners to cry out, 'Blessed be the God and Father of our Lord Jesus Christ, who has blessed us in Christ with every spiritual blessing in the heavenly places, even as he chose us in him before the foundation of the world, that we should be holy and blameless before him' (Eph. 1:3-4a).

Election is always known by the transformation it effects in a person's life. Where moral and spiritual transformation is absent, election to life is not present. Above all else, the grace of election produces humility before God and adoration of God. What do we have that we did not first receive? (cf. 1 Cor. 4:7-8). It is this truth that lies at the heart of the Christian believer's assurance. Nowhere do the Scriptures display this truth more eloquently than in Romans 8:28-39. Since God works all things for the good of those who are called according to his purpose (verse 28); and since no one can bring any charge against God's elect (verse 33); and since no one can condemn us because Christ Jesus died, was raised, and is now at God's right hand interceding for us, Paul can draw the glorious conclusion, 'Who shall separate us from the love of Christ?' His answer is that nothing and no one 'will be able to separate us from the love of God in Christ Jesus our Lord'. God's electing love, his wholly gracious and ill-deserved love, in Christ, is the solid ground on which our faith rests. Our faith may rise and fall; but the Lord's love is unfailing. He loved and chose us from before the first of time; he will love us and preserve us to and beyond the last. *Soli Deo Gloria.*

35. The Spirit and Practice of Sabbath-Keeping: Enjoying Gospel Rest

Mention the word 'Sabbath' and many Christians immediately think of the Old Testament and the many rules and regulations that surrounded the fourth commandment. It is assumed that with the coming of Jesus and the de-nationalising and subsequent internationalising of the church, the fourth commandment has been abrogated and no longer features in the lifestyle of the individual Christian and of the church as a whole. What is often forgotten, however, is that the Sabbath day predates the Ten Commandments (Gen. 2:2-3). Before it was a Mosaic and Jewish ordinance, the Sabbath was a creational ordinance. Indeed, the fourth commandment assumed, not inaugurated, the Sabbath day: 'Remember the Sabbath day, to keep it holy' (Exod. 20:8-11). From the dawn of history, God instituted the Sabbath day and wove it into the essential rhythm of his creation. It would be surprising then if God would abandon the rhythm of his creation by abrogating the Sabbath day. Certainly, as we will see, the temporary Jewish character of the Sabbath has been abrogated, but not the Sabbath itself.

It is a sad fact that Sabbath-keeping has often been for many Christians a joyless, dreary experience and not the joyful, renewing experience it ought to be and was intended to be. How is it possible for godly Sabbath-keeping to be joyless and dreary, when God himself rested on the Sabbath day and our Sabbath-keeping is to be patterned after his?

The aim of this chapter is to so present the Bible's teaching on Sabbath-keeping that the reader's spiritual appetite to keep the Sabbath day holy, that is, set apart to the Lord, will be whetted.

First, we need to be alert to an ever-present danger. In biblical, that is, God-revealed religion, we are confronted again and again with a devilish danger. We see this danger graphically and grotesquely pictured for us in Isaiah 1:10-20. God's privileged and covenant people were punctilious in their religious observance. They did all that the law of God commanded them to do, but they did it self-righteously. They prided themselves on their religious duteousness. Their religion, orthodox and biblical as to its forms and requirements, was smug, self-satisfied, and legalistic. Let me be clear: legalism has nothing to do, as such, with keeping God's commandments. Jesus said, 'If you love me, you will keep my commandments' (John 14:15); and the apostle John wrote, 'and his commandments are not burdensome' (1 John 5:3; read also 1 John 2:3-4). What then is legalism? It is a devilish spirit, a spirit that prides itself in 'doing' rather than in 'believing'. Legalism is law-keeping divorced from love to the great law-giver. Legalism is law-keeping with a snooty nose, not with a humble heart. The spirit of legalism says, 'Look at me; see how good I am', whereas the spirit of godly law-keeping says, 'Look at Christ; see how great he is.'

Now, even well-taught Reformed Christians are not exempt from this devilish spirit. Through Isaiah, God is addressing his chosen, covenant people, his church, saying to them (with all their vast privileges), 'I cannot endure your Sabbath-keeping, and your appointed feasts—I hate them' (see Isa. 1:13-14). But God himself had appointed and commanded them! Yes, but they were never intended to be ends in themselves. They were 'holy means', sanctified means, by which God would meet with his people in his grace and enrich their lives.

This unholy formalism and mere duteousness is also found in the new covenant church. In 1 Corinthians 11:17-34, Paul rebukes the church in Corinth for the unholy, self-willed arrogance that was defacing and defiling the celebration of the Lord's Supper. The inauguration of the new covenant did not immunise the church from 'serpentine' behaviour. Throughout its history, the church has been afflicted with the creeping and insidious presence of formalism. Jesus' words in Mark 7:6-7 should ever inform the private and corporate worship and service of believers. Quoting Isaiah 29:13, Jesus said, 'This people honours me with their lips, but their heart is far from me.'

Second, having highlighted the great and ever-present danger of unholy formalism, we need now to ask, in what spirit are we to keep the Sabbath day holy?

First, *we are to keep the Sabbath as dependent creatures* (Exod. 20:8-11). Every Sabbath day, the Christian Lord's day, we are summoned to re-set our lives under the Lordship of Almighty God. Yes, we do this every day; but in his great kindness the Lord has given us a special day in which to do this 'undistractedly'. Every resurrection morning, the Christian believer rises to confess that he/she is not living in a mindless cosmos, that we are not cosmic accidents, but creatures of the living God. All things everywhere were made by him and we are his creatures. The day reminds us that in the beginning he made all things 'very good'. The world we see and are part of is not the world God made; it has gone bad. The creational Sabbath was a continual reminder to Adam that history is not a ceaseless repetition of days. The 'weekly cycle impressed on him that he, together with the created order as a whole, was moving toward a goal, a nothing less than eschatological culmination' (Richard B. Gaffin).

The Christian Sabbath (or rest) then summons us to the highest of all activities—*worship*—in which we find and will ultimately find our eternal rest.

Second, *we are to keep the Sabbath as redeemed sinners* (Deut. 5:15). The Sabbath day pictures for us the 'finished work' of Christ in redeeming sinners. It should not surprise us that Christians set apart the Lord's day, the day of resurrection, as their Sabbath day. The creational Sabbath was the culmination of God's work of creation; the new covenant Sabbath is the inauguration of God's work of redemption. Every Lord's day we are reminded that we are not our own, that we have been bought with a price.

Third, *we are to keep the Sabbath as pilgrim saints*. The Sabbath is a weekly sign of our present pilgrimage. Every Lord's day, the Lord is telling us, 'You are not home yet.' Christians are a pilgrim people. We live here, but 'our citizenship is in heaven' (Phil. 3:20).

Our Lord's words in Matthew 11:28-30 are of some importance in this regard. The word Jesus uses here for 'rest' is *anapausō*, which was a virtual synonym for Sabbath (we get our word 'pause' from it). Jesus is saying, 'The rest that was promised and held out in creation and Exodus can only be found in me.' The Resurrection Sabbath is therefore not the final rest. There yet remains a Sabbath rest for the people of God, the final Sabbath. Just as the Lord's Supper combines elements of memorial and expectation—remembering his death and anticipating his coming—so the Lord's day gathers up all that has gone before and looks for that which is yet to come. The point of the writer to the Hebrews is that there 'remains' a Sabbath rest for the people of God (Heb. 4:9), and to this truth the weekly Sabbath/Lord's day points.

Fourth, *we are to keep the Sabbath day 'holily'*. In setting the day apart, we are to remember that the Resurrection Sabbath we celebrate is not the Exodus Sabbath. As Bruce Ray reminds us, 'That Sabbath, with its ceremonies and sacrifices, died with Christ and rose again on the first day of the week as the Lord's day of the New Covenant.'

The relationship between the old covenant and the new covenant is not one of absolute identity, but of progressive continuity. This means that while the specific day and form of Sabbath observance has changed in the New Testament, the principle of Sabbath-keeping remains basic to biblical faith and life. The Christian church is God's multi-national, multi-cultural family. At Pentecost the church burst out of the womb of Judaism; the temporary scaffolding of Jewish ritual was taken down (Gal. 3–4). The Christian Sabbath is not identical to the Mosaic Sabbath—how could it be? We receive the Sabbath from Jesus Christ, 'the Lord of the Sabbath' (Mark 2:28), and not from Moses—just as the Mosaic Sabbath was a God-ordained development of the creational Sabbath, temporarily demarcating and defining the life of God's old covenant people.

Fifth, *we are to keep the Sabbath day happily*. The Sabbath worship of God's people should above all be characterised by joy (Psa. 100). Of course there will be confession. But the dominant note should be one of joy, exuberance, delight. It is always a delight to spend time with the people we love!

Finally, *we are to keep the Sabbath day recreationally.* The Sabbath is a time for recreation, in mind, in body, in spirit. This has been much misunderstood. When we read in Isaiah 58:13-14, 'If you turn back your foot from the Sabbath, from doing your pleasure on my holy day, and call the Sabbath a delight and the holy day of the LORD honourable; if you honour it, not going your own ways, or seeking your own pleasure, or talking idly; then you shall take delight in the LORD, and I will make you ride on the heights of the earth; I will feed you with the heritage of Jacob your father, for the mouth of the LORD has spoken', does 'going your own ways' and 'seeking your own pleasure' refer to those things you enjoy doing? For example, if you enjoy walking, or talking with your children or wife, are you to cease from doing those on the Sabbath day? Surely the Lord is speaking here of 'wilfulness', rather than recreation as such. The point of the passage is not that you avoid doing anything you enjoy or find pleasurable, but that you 'take every thought captive to obey Christ' (2 Cor. 10:5). There must be a measure of freedom here. We are all different.

In his excellent defence and exposition of the new covenant Sabbath, *Call the Sabbath a Delight,*[1] Walt Chantry

---

[1] Walter J. Chantry, *Call the Sabbath a Delight* (Edinburgh: Banner of Truth Trust, 1991).

uses this example: Your children might love riding bicycles every day, so you say to them, 'On Sunday we will leave our bicycles aside to help us make the day different.' But a Christian neighbour, whose children are not so keen on riding bikes, may say, 'Let us go on a bike ride for exercise and to spend time together.' The legalistic mind will say, 'If I cannot jog, or walk or ride a bike and keep the Sabbath holy, then neither can any of my brothers!' We are not to legislate the particulars of Sabbath-keeping; but we are to keep the Sabbath day holy, that is, unto the Lord.

There is a danger in giving the Sabbath such a central place in Christian living. Sabbath-keeping, as we have seen, can become a self-righteous exercise. But it was our Lord Jesus Christ who said, 'If you love me, you will keep my commandments' (John 14:15).

The keeping of the Lord's day, the Christian Sabbath, can be the result of either legal obedience or evangelical obedience. Where it is the product of legal obedience, Sabbath-keeping will be joyless, routine, formal, and self-congratulatory. But where Sabbath-keeping is the fruit of evangelical obedience, it will be deeply joyful. We will say with the Psalmist, 'I was glad when they said to me, "Let us go to the house of the LORD!"' (Psa. 122:1). When we keep the Sabbath out of evangelical obedience, it is refreshing, invigorating, and self-humbling.

John Murray (whom I often quote, not just because he was a Scotsman, but because his writings made an indelible impression on me as a young Christian) says this about the

Sabbath: 'The weekly Sabbath is the promise, token and foretaste of the consummated rest. The biblical philosophy of the Sabbath is such that to deny its perpetuity is to deprive the movement of redemption of one of its most precious strands.'

We live in a day when more than ever we need to recover the Sabbath for God's people. Because we love the people of God, we long for their good before God, and the good that God longs to bless his people with will never come to them apart from them honouring his holy day. For the spiritual good of our children we need to raise them to honour the day of the Lord, not as something dull and routine and formal. How could the worship of God, waiting on God, talking and thinking about the Lord Jesus Christ, be dull and formal?

Let me give the last word to Richard Baxter: 'What fitter day to ascend to heaven than that on which he arose from the earth and fully triumphed over death and hell. Use your Sabbaths as steps to glory till you have passed them all and are there arrived.'

36. Less than the Least:
The Soil of Gospel Usefulness

How can Christians live useful lives? How can we live lives that God can safely use to advance his kingdom? Ephesians 3:8 highlights the 'secret', the open secret, of Paul's and all Christian usefulness: 'To me, though I am the very least of all the saints, this grace was given, to preach to the Gentiles the unsearchable riches of Christ.' Paul was a man overwhelmed both by a deep sense of his own personal unfitness and the greatness and glory of the gospel.

First, he had a deep sense of his own unfitness. He says he is 'the very least of all the saints'. Not, 'I *was*', but, 'I *am*'. Paul had no inflated sense of his spiritual capacities. He actually uses the comparative, *elachistoteros*, and not the superlative, *elachistos*, literally, 'to me who am the leaster of all the saints'. Why this manifest lapse in grammar? Paul is a man deeply humbled by the astonishing privilege God had given to him. He calls himself 'less than the least'. Usefulness to God grows in the soil of self-effacing humility. Humility is the 'disposition of honest recognition' (Albert N. Martin). The humble are not a personality type, but a spiritual type. They are the 'poor in spirit' (Matt. 5:3). They can never get over the astonishing privilege of God saving them in Christ and calling them to serve Christ. They may well be extrovert, even loud, but they always, *always*, ALWAYS, give God the glory. God will not use men or women who think they are anything. I don't mean we are ever to deny that we have brains or gifts or abilities, but we must have 1 Corinthians 4:7-8 branded on our hearts and minds—we must be men and women who understand that we are debtors to mercy alone.

It was Paul's overwhelming sense of his personal unworthiness and the no less overwhelming wonder of his call to be a minister of the unsearchable riches of Christ that made him lapse in his grammar. Gospel not grammar was Paul's obsession.

Second, he has a deep sense of the gospel's greatness. Paul writes of 'the unsearchable riches of Christ'. Throughout his long ministerial life, the gospel never became *passé*, or commonplace or routine for Paul. It was always an inexhaustible treasure, a bottomless deep. Søren Kierkegaard said life was seventy thousand fathoms deep. I wonder if any of us think of the gospel like that? Seventy thousand fathoms deep. How deep can you dive? One, two, perhaps three fathoms? Seventy thousand fathoms. The gospel of Christ is a bottomless deep. Why? Because the Lord Jesus Christ is himself a bottomless deep. He is the gospel (1 Cor. 1:30; Luke 2:29-32).

Every Christian and certainly every Christian minister is called to be a deep-sea diver. It is the Christian minister's vast privilege to pull up treasure after treasure, week by week, and set it before God's people. Herman Bavinck wrote that the fundamental idea in Christian theology is the incomprehensibility of God.[1] He meant that no matter how hard and how long we read and think and preach, we are still beginners, we never arrive; how can we!

Christian ministers are called to be lifelong explorers and divers. The more we explore and dive, the more we discover how sinful we are and how great and glorious the gospel of God is.

Some years ago I read these words of James Denney and wished I had read them as a young theological student: 'No man can give at once the impression that he himself is clever and that Jesus Christ is mighty to save.'[2] It is the gospel of the God of grace that knocks the pride out of us. That we who deserve God's just and righteous judgment should be given the privilege of making known the unsearchable riches of Christ is a wonder, a great wonder. Understanding this and feeling the wonder of it is the soil out of which usefulness in God's kingdom grows.

[1] *Reformed Dogmatics*, II.39.
[2] James Denney, quoted in James S. Stewart, *Heralds of God* (New York, 1946), p. 74.

37. *Samuel Rutherford:*
Gospel-Shaped Spirituality

When the gospel of God invades our lives, it plants within us the seed of a new life, 'God's seed' (1 John 3:9). This new life is deeply idiosyncratic. There is nothing stereotypical or monochrome about the Christian life. And yet this new life has identifiable features that will be found in the lives of all God's children.

Samuel Rutherford's legacy to the Christian church is immense. There is little doubt, however, that his greatest legacy was his letters. The spirituality and piety of his letters give the lie that Calvinism is cold, hard, or clinical. Whatever else it is, Calvinism, as we see from Rutherford's letters, is warm, evangelical, deeply affectional and others-centred religion. Cold Calvinism is a theological oxymoron!

Throughout his letters a number of themes surface again and again, themes which are, in every age, the hallmarks of evangelical, gospel piety.

1. *Gospel spirituality is supremely Christocentric.* Jesus Christ is the thematic centrepiece of Rutherford's letters. Consider the note struck in the following selection:

> Give Christ your virgin love; you cannot put your love and heart into better hand. Oh! If ye knew Him, and saw His beauty, your love, your liking,

> your heart, your desires would close with Him and cleave to Him. ... O fair sun, and fair moon and fair stars, and fair flowers, and fair roses, and fair lilies and fair creatures, but O ten thousand thousand times fairer Lord Jesus.[1]

> Christ is a well of life; but who knoweth how deep it is to the bottom? ... And oh, what a fair one, what an only one, what an excellent, lovely, ravishing one is Jesus.[2]

The majesty and loveliness of Christ is the outstanding theme of his letters:

> Oh, but Christ is heaven's wonder, and earth's wonder! What marvel that His bride saith, 'He is altogether lovely', ... Oh, pity for evermore, that there should be such a one as Christ Jesus, so boundless, so bottomless, and so incomparable in infinite excellency and sweetness and so few to take him.[3]

2. Gospel spirituality has a deep concern for the undying souls of men and women. Rutherford saw people in the light of eternity. He had a passionate care for their eternal wellbeing, which is a marked characteristic of Puritan piety and of the Reformed pastor.

---

[1] To the Laird of Cally, 1637.
[2] To Lady Hilconquar, 8 August 1637.
[3] *Ibid.*

Thoughts of your soul depart not from me in my sleep. ... Oh, if I could buy your soul's salvation with any suffering whatsoever, that ye and I might meet with joy up in the rainbow, when we shall stand before our Judge.[1]

My witness is above; your heaven would be two heavens to me, and your salvation two salvations.[2]

In this deep concern for the souls of men and women, Rutherford was merely exemplifying a common feature of the Reformed pastor and, more importantly, the Lord Jesus Christ himself (cf. Luke 19:41-42; Paul in Rom. 9:1-3; 10:1).

3. *Gospel spirituality has a deep sense of the sinfulness of sin.* Like all truly biblically taught men, Rutherford was most conscious of his own sin. He was perpetually conscious of his own 'abominable vileness': 'Only my loathsome wretchedness and my wants have qualified me for Christ' (cf. 1 Tim. 1:15; Eph. 3:8).

It deeply troubled Rutherford that one so depraved should be admired as a master of the spiritual life. The truth surely, however, is that only those who have such a deep, Spirit-persuaded sense of their sinfulness before God can be effective ministers of God's truth to others! Only someone who knows his own heart before God can begin to understand another. 'Ye are as near heaven as ye are far from yourself.'

[1] To Gordon of Cardoness, 16 June 1637.
[2] To the church in Anwoth, 13 July 1632.

4. *Gospel spirituality ministers comfort to fellow believers*. Tender compassion and strong counsel are distinguishing features throughout the letters. To Vicountess Kenmure, who was suffering spiritual depression, Rutherford wrote:

> Never believe that your tenderhearted Saviour, who knoweth the strength of your stomach, will mix that cup with one dram-weight of poison. Drink then with the patience of the saints, and the God of patience bless your medicine.[1]

Rutherford's profound spiritual counsel has been cherished over the centuries, perhaps above all because he wrote out of deep personal sufferings and anguish:

> My wife is so tormented night and day, that I have wondered why the Lord tarrieth so long. My life is bitter unto me ... it is hard to keep sight of God in a storm.[2]

His own family circumstances, and sore exile, gave him, in God's grace, a fellow feeling with afflicted Christians. His spiritual counsel was not formed in the study; it was forged in the sore trials that a sovereign and loving providence brought into his life.

5. *Gospel spirituality is full of eagerness for heaven*. The centre of Rutherford's life lay in heaven, not on earth:

---

[1] Letter of 27 July 1628.
[2] To Marion McNaught, 17 Nov. 1629.

Oh, when will we meet! Oh, how long is it to the dawning of the marriage day! O sweet Jesus, take wide steps! O my Lord, come over the mountain at one stride.[1]

O fairest among sons of men, why stayest Thou so long away? O heaven move fast! O time run, run, and hasten the marriage day.[2]

For Rutherford, Jesus Christ was everything! In this, Rutherford exemplified the heart of true Calvinism: to live for the glory of God, to love and serve the Lord Jesus Christ, to do good to God's people. This is true gospel spirituality. It is not wrapped up in itself. Gospel spirituality, or piety, does not neglect to look out for and to care for other Christians, especially those in need. Rutherford's letters were written in the main to his own parishioners and to other Christians who sought out his counsel. This is why gospel spirituality is nourished most within the life of the church.

Our piety will only truly deepen when we sink our lives into the fellowship of Christ's church, which is, after all, his body, the body of which every Christian is a living member.

---

[1] To John Gordon of Cardoness, 16 June 1637.
[2] To Earlston the Younger, 16 June 1637.

38. Lyrical Beauty from Augustine: Gospel Ecstasy

Augustine's *Confessions* is a 300-page prose prayer. It is a stunning piece of spiritual literature. There is barely a page that does not contain a sentence, phrase or paragraph that immediately compels attention. Most Christians know perhaps the section where he recounts his conversion in the garden in Milan. In prayer he recounts the story of his conversion to God, overjoyed with wondering thankfulness. But this note of wondering thankfulness pervades almost the whole book, especially the latter half, where he reflects prayerfully on the grace of God's love to him in Christ.

There is one passage that especially stands out both for its lyrical beauty and its affectional spirituality:

> My love for you, Lord, is not an uncertain feeling but a matter of conscious certainty. ... But when I love you, what do I love? It is not physical beauty nor temporal glory nor the brightness of light dear to earthly eyes, nor the sweet melodies of all kinds of songs, nor the gentle odour of flowers and oint- ments and perfumes, nor manna or honey, nor limbs welcoming the embraces of the flesh; it is not these I love when I love my God. Yet there is a light I love, and a food, and a kind of embrace when I

love my God—a light, voice, odour, food, embrace of the inner man, where my soul is floodlit by light which space cannot contain, where there is sound that time cannot seize, where there is a perfume which no breeze disperses, where there is a taste for food no amount of eating can lessen, and where there is a bond of union that no satiety can part. That is what I love when I love my God.

I am not sure what my response should be to such Samuel Rutherford-like spiritual ecstasy. Perhaps the best response is one of awed silence and internal reflection. Jonathan Edwards never wearied of telling his congregation in Northampton, Massachusetts, that true religion consists in spiritual affections. Edwards, and before him Rutherford and Augustine, was simply echoing the teaching of God's word. True religion, that is, the religion revealed in the Bible, the religion that originates in the Holy Trinity and finds its centre point and omega point in Jesus Christ, is natively experiential and affectional. It could hardly be otherwise. If the gospel, by the grace and power of the Holy Spirit, unites us to Christ, we become, in some measure, partakers of his life. He is the vine and we are the branches (John 15:1-4). His life is our life; indeed he is our life (Col. 3:4).

It is because the Lord Jesus Christ is our life that the Christian life cannot be affectionless, or mundane, or always even. There will necessarily be times of heightened outgoings of love to, and delight in, the Saviour. As it was with the Master, so it will be, must be, with the Master's servants. There were times in Jesus' earthly life when his humanity was punctuated with moments of heightened spirituality—think of his baptism and his transfiguration. So it will be, or should be, with Christians. Most of our life will be a steady, sure, unspectacular walk of faith. But there will be moments when heaven comes down and glory fills our souls, to borrow words from the hymn-writer.

Let me now ask what may be a surprising question: Where and when will these heightened spiritual moments be experienced? For many Christians the answer is obvious: wherever and whenever we hold our 'quiet times'. Regular, even daily, times of Bible reading and prayer are vital to the Christian's growth in grace. Times of family worship are also occasions when God will bless our souls and deepen our grasp of the glory of Christ. But should we not expect the public worship of God's children, on the day he has commanded, to be the occasion when we most enjoy occasions of heightened spiritual experience?

This conviction may run counter to the incipient individualism that has so scarred the face of evangelical Christianity in recent decades. The rapidly declining attendance at the evening service on the Lord's day, in many evangelical and even Reformed churches, is a devastating indication of how low a priority the public gatherings of God's people are for many professing Christians.

The writer of the letter to the Hebrews commands his readers not to neglect meeting together (Heb. 10:25). Why?

Because he knows that to do so is a revealing symptom of a spiritually debilitated Christian. The public worship services of God's people on the Lord's day are a foretaste of that endless service of worship that believers will enjoy together throughout the ages of eternity. Heaven will not be populated with myriads of Christians holding private communion with God. No. Rather, we will employ our unique contribution to the endless praise of the glorified church around God's throne.

Ought we not to prepare for that day by taking every opportunity to gather with our Christian brothers and sisters, using, as Richard Baxter put it, 'our Sabbaths as stepping-stones to glory, until having passed them all, we are there arrived'?

39. *Thomas Goodwin: Gospel Assurance*

Thomas Goodwin was a remarkable Christian. He was a pre-eminent pastor-theologian and a deeply insightful expositor of God's word. Alexander Whyte thought he was the greatest-ever expositor of Paul's letters. But Goodwin was first and foremost a Christian. It was because he knew in measure his own heart and because of the struggles he experienced in his early years to find assurance of faith that Goodwin could write so pastorally and empathetically to fellow believers.

Goodwin struggled for many years to possess a personal assurance of saving faith. Through the counsel of a godly minister, Mr Price of King's Lynn, he was led to see his need to 'live by faith in Christ, and to derive from him life and strength for sanctification, and all comfort and joy through believing'. Goodwin later wrote of these years:

> I was diverted from Christ for several years, to search only into the signs of grace in me. It was almost seven years ere I was taken off to live by faith on Christ, and God's free love, which are alike the object of faith.[1]

Goodwin's experience of God's grace has much to teach us: above all, that the believer's primary focus is Christ, not himself. 'I am come to this pass now', wrote Goodwin to Mr Price, 'that signs will do me no good alone; I have trusted too much to habitual grace for assurance of salvation; I tell you Christ is worth all.'[2]

In *Christ Set Forth* (recently republished by the Banner of Truth),[3] Goodwin seeks to persuade us that we find assurance first, and supremely, and in a sense only, by looking to Christ and trusting in him and his finished

---

[1] *Works of Thomas Goodwin* (Edinburgh: James Nichol, 1861), II.58 (lxviii).

[2] *Ibid.*, lxx.

[3] Thomas Goodwin, *Christ Set Forth* (Edinburgh: Banner of Truth Trust, 2015).

work on the cross. Looking inwards to ourselves to find crumbs to encourage us that we are in Christ is, according to Goodwin, a fruitless and utterly dispiriting and futile exercise. He is not saying that we should not be encouraged by the presence of God's grace in our lives. He is saying, however, that too many Christians 'in the ordinary course and way of their spirits have been too much carried away with the rudiments of Christ in their own hearts, and not after Christ himself'.[1]

Goodwin develops this conviction in a number of soul-stirring and soul-encouraging ways. What follows is one of the ways Goodwin seeks to turn us away from ourselves to look out to Christ. Let us, he writes:

> see what matter of support and encouragement faith may fetch from Christ's death for justification. And surely that which hath long ago satisfied God himself for the sins of many thousand souls now in heaven, may very well serve to satisfy the heart and conscience of any sinner now upon earth, in any doubts in respect of the guilt of any sins that can arise.[2]

Do you grasp what Goodwin is saying? Our sins rise to condemn us. Our sins are many and not few. Our sins are wicked and deserving of God's just condemnation. What good can be gained by looking into ourselves? What do

[1] *Christ Set Forth*, p. xv.
[2] *Ibid.*, p. 43.

you see when you look into yourself? Paul told us what he saw: 'O wretched man that I am!' (Rom. 7:24 KJV). There is no comfort to be found looking in; we must learn to look out to Christ. The sin-bearing, sin-atoning death of Christ satisfied God. He accepted the Saviour's sacrifice in our place, as our covenant head. He accepted the sacrifice. He was satisfied with his sacrifice. Now, Goodwin is saying to us, if God is satisfied, should you not also be satisfied? If all your sins were laid on God's own Son and were forever put behind God's back, buried in the deepest sea and remembered no more, should that not be your assurance? (Mic. 7:19; Isa. 43:25).

The great tendency of sin, as Martin Luther never wearied of saying, is to turn us into ourselves ('*incurvatus in se*'). The great tendency of the gospel is to turn us away from ourselves and to set our gaze fully and alone on our great Saviour. Our hope before God does not rest in any particle of righteousness within. All our hope lies in what the Reformers called 'an alien righteousness', a righteousness found outside of ourselves in Jesus Christ. This is what Paul tells us in 1 Corinthians 1:30: Christ 'became to us wisdom from God, righteousness and sanctification and redemption'.

Jesus Christ is our assurance. Yes, our God-planted graces may, through the lens of Christ (never apart from him), bring us a measure of comfort. But our graces ebb and flow, they rise and fall, they are here today and all but gone tomorrow. No wonder Paul cried out, 'O wretched man that I am!' But 'Jesus Christ is the same yesterday and today and for ever' (Heb. 13:8). He is at God's right hand. He is our justification and our eternal acceptance with God (Rom. 8:34).

Listen again to Goodwin: 'Were any of your duties crucified for you?' He is addressing a recurring tendency even in godly Christians to look into themselves for 'signs', here signs that we are faithful in evangelical duties. (This further question could no less be asked: Were any of your graces crucified for you?) Goodwin's question is plain but profound. Don't look in, look out to your crucified Saviour who alone is your righteousness. 'Therefore', says Goodwin, 'get your hearts and consciences distinctly and particularly satisfied in the all-sufficiency of worth and merit which is in the satisfaction that Christ hath made.'[1] For Goodwin, the Christian's great need is to grasp what he calls the transcendent all-sufficiency of Christ's death.

This is no abstractly doctrinal concern. Goodwin looks ahead to the day of Christ:

> Now you will all be thus called one day to dispute for your souls, sooner or later; and therefore such skill you should endeavour to get in Christ's righteousness, how in its fullness and perfection it answereth to all your sinfulness.[2]

Is this not pastoral theology at its purest and most practical? The doctrine of the gospel is itself, in all its

[1] *Ibid.*, p. 50.
[2] *Ibid.*, p. 51.

multi-facetedness, the balm, support and encouragement for which our hearts cry out. So the writer to the
Hebrews all but concludes his brief word of exhortation
(Heb. 13:22) with the words, 'let us run with endurance
the race that is set before us, looking [away] to Jesus, the
founder and perfecter of our faith' (12:1-2). *Looking away
to Jesus* is the constant gaze of the believing life. Anything
other would indicate a distempered mind or a lukewarm
or cold heart. Make Christ dying the object of your faith.

40. 'The Crook in the Lot': Gospel Living in a Fallen World

Those of you who know even a little about a remarkable eighteenth-century Scottish minister called
Thomas Boston will have immediately recognised the
source of my title.

Boston's *Works* run to twelve volumes and contain some
lengthy theological treatises. When Jonathan Edwards read
Boston's work on the Covenants, he said that the Scottish minister was 'a truly great divine'. But Boston also
wrote brief, very accessible and pastoral books, and chief
among these is the quaintly titled, *The Crook in the Lot*,
with the subtitle, *The Sovereignty and Wisdom of God,
in the Afflictions of Men Displayed*. This little book (168

pages in the Banner of Truth Puritan Paperback edition),
is a pastoral masterpiece, in which Boston reflects on the
words of the Preacher in Ecclesiastes 7:13: 'Consider the
work of God: for who can make that straight which he
hath made crooked?' (KJV).

Thomas Boston was born in 1676 at a time when vital
religion often suffered the fires of persecution. His father
had been imprisoned for his steadfast commitment to the
doctrines of the Reformed faith. Boston's *Memoirs* (a must-
read) recount the many crooks that affected his own lot
in life as a faithful minister of the grace of God. His wife
suffered physical and mental infirmity for many years and
he buried six of his ten children. He died in 1732, the year
before the first secession from the Church of Scotland.

Boston was a remarkable pastor/scholar. When he began
his new ministry in Ettrick, about forty miles south of
Edinburgh, in 1707, sixty people came to the Lord's Table.
In 1731, 777 communicated at the Table. John 'Rabbi'
Duncan said that he wished he could send his students
to Jonathan Edwards to hear what true gospel godliness
was; and then send them to Thomas Boston to discover
how to get it!

Before I let Boston speak for himself, let me explain
what he means by 'crook' and 'lot'. By 'lot', Boston means
our 'lot in life', the shape of our lives as they are styled
by God's many providences. By 'crook', he means those
unforeseen troubles ('thorns') that afflict, unsettle or dis-
turb us in any way. Boston sets out to minister pastoral

wisdom and help to God's people experiencing crooks in their lots, what Paul calls 'the sufferings of this present time' (Rom. 8:18).

As Boston begins to unpack his text, he does so in the form of 'three propositions':

First Proposition: 'Whatsoever crook there is in one's lot, it is of God's making.' Boston wants his readers to understand that

> Everybody's lot in this world hath some crook in it. Complainers are apt to make odious comparisons: they look about, and taking a distant view of the condition of others, can discern nothing in it but what is straight, and just to one's wish; so they pronounce their neighbour's lot wholly straight.

But, says Boston, that is a false verdict; 'there is no perfection here, no lot out of heaven without a crook'.

Boston is highlighting a very basic, but very important, truth. Life this side of glory is marred by inescapable crooks. This is true for everyone everywhere, and not least for God's chosen, saved and heaven-bound children.

It is one of the devil's stratagems to try to persuade us that other people don't have the crooks in their lot that we have. Comparisons truly are odious. You and I never really know what is going on in anyone's life (we barely know what is going on most of the time in our own lives). Living in a fallen world, in yet fallen bodies, with sin's entail yet within us, crooks in the lot are an inevitable part of life.

But more to Boston's point is his assertion that all of our crooks are 'of God's making'. God's sovereignty is absolutely unabridged (Eph. 1:11). It may often be dark and mysterious to us, but it is the wise, kind, gracious, if always just, sovereignty of our heavenly Father—the Father who spared not his only Son for us.

Second Proposition: 'What God sees meet [appropriate] to mar, no one shall be able to mend in his lot.' Boston is not meaning that we should simply shrug our shoulders and say (with Doris Day), '*Que sera, sera*' when the Lord is pleased to send crooks into our lot. What he means is that by our own strength or ability we cannot mend the crooks in our lot. If they are to be mended, it will be the Lord who mends them. We should pray and even plead. But it will be the Lord himself who removes the crooks, if they are ever to be removed this side of glory. Boston has much to say on this, but he says one thing that is very needful: 'If you would, in a Christian manner, set yourselves to bear the crook, you would find it easier than you imagine.' He then quotes Jesus' words: 'Take my yoke upon you, and learn from me ... and you will find rest for your souls. For my yoke is easy, and my burden is light' (Matt. 11:29-30). Like Samuel Rutherford in the previous century, Boston was wholly taken up with the Lord Jesus Christ. He was always encouraging his congregation to 'go to Christ'.

Third Proposition: 'The considering the crook in the lot as the work of God is a proper means to bring one to behave rightly under it.' Boston proceeds to ask the question, How are Christians to behave when it pleases the Lord to bring various crooks into their lives? His answer is simple: 'Better it is to be of an humble spirit with the lowly, than to divide the spoil with the proud' (Prov. 16:19 KJV). Boston proceeds to tell us that 'Humility is part of the image of God. Pride is the masterpiece of the image of the devil.' He reminds us that 'Though the LORD be high, yet hath he respect unto the lowly: but the proud he knoweth afar off' (Psa. 138:6 KJV). So when crooks appear in your life, listen and take to heart Peter's words: '"God opposes the proud but gives grace to the humble." Humble yourselves, therefore, under the mighty hand of God so that at the proper time he may exalt you, casting all your anxieties on him, because he cares for you' (1 Pet. 5:6-7).

Perhaps the most remarkable feature of Boston's *Crook in the Lot* is the fact that over half the book is devoted to explicating and applying this one fundamental response Christians must seek to cultivate as they face their God-sent crooks. Nothing is more vital than cultivating the grace of humility. Humility is receiving and meekly accepting all that the Lord pleases to bring into our lives, for good or for ill. For Boston, Jesus is our model and pattern. Not once in the face of all the many crooks that afflicted his lot did our Saviour murmur or complain. His one invariable response to crooks in his lot was, 'It is the Lord.'

So, unsurprisingly, Boston concludes his little pastoral gem with a final exhortative encouragement:

Ye have been called to humble yourselves in your humbling circumstances, and have been assured in that case of a lifting up. To conclude: we may assure ourselves, God will at length break in pieces the proud, be they ever so high; and he will triumphantly lift up the humble, be they ever so low.

The Crook in the Lot is pastoral medicine prepared in the laboratory of Boston's own personal and ministerial sufferings. It is little wonder that Jonathan Edwards considered Boston 'a truly great divine'. He was.

41. *When I Don't Feel Forgiven: How the Gospel Gives Us Comfort*

The Christian life is a constant battle against the world, the flesh and the devil. If this unholy trinity had its way, it would destroy every single one of God's blood-bought and dearly loved children. But as our Lord Jesus assures us, not one of those for whom he shed his precious blood will be lost. Nothing and no one can snatch a Christian, even the weakest Christian, from the strong hands of our omnipotent heavenly Father. Our eternal security is guaranteed by our union with Christ. This is gloriously and unassailably true. But this glorious truth does not mean that our Christian lives cannot be disturbed, even deeply disturbed, by the unholy trinity of the world, the flesh and the devil.

Perhaps the most disturbing experience a believer can face is losing the felt sense of God's forgiveness. This desolating experience has touched the lives of many Christians throughout the ages. It can happen 'all of a sudden'. In Ephesians 6:16, Paul writes about 'the flaming darts of the evil one', sudden, perhaps unexpected assaults on our standing in Christ. Or it may be that the loss of the felt sense of God's forgiveness happens slowly over a period of time. Whether suddenly or slowly, this is a desolating experience for any Christian to go through. What are believers to do when they do not feel forgiven?

First, they are to undertake *gospel self-examination*. When we do not feel forgiven, we must ask ourselves if we are harbouring sin in our hearts. Sin natively dulls our hearts and minds to God's grace in his Son. There may be a good and godly reason why we do not feel our Father's forgiving love. It may be that our ever-gracious God is removing the sense of our Christ-won comforts from us in order to awaken us to the sin we are refusing to put to death in our members (Rom. 8:13). The words of Psalm 139:23-24 should never be far from our thoughts: 'Search me, O God, and know my heart! Try me and know my thoughts! And see if there be any grievous way in me, and lead me in the way everlasting.' This was a note the writer to the Hebrews highlighted to his hard-pressed, spiritually debilitated readers (Heb. 12:5-6).

Second, we are to engage in *gospel realism*. When we do not feel forgiven, we must remind ourselves that we are engaged in a relentless warfare with the world, the flesh and the devil. The devil will use every strategy he can devise to rob us of our gospel comforts, turn us in upon ourselves, and so overwhelm us with our circumstances that God seems far off and even heartlessly unconcerned about our sad spiritual state. The word of God never hides from us the potential costliness of faithful discipleship. In Isaiah 50:10, God's prophet addresses the Messiah's servants who walk in darkness and have no light. It is hard to imagine what it must be like to be a true believer and yet be so overwhelmed with 'darkness' that not even a pinprick of light penetrates the utter gloom. This, of course, was the experience of the proto-typical man of faith, our Saviour Jesus Christ. All the lights went out in his life, not because he was a disobedient Son but because he was a perfectly obedient Son. The Lord never promises that the life of faith will be a life of unbroken, unsullied communion with him. The godly life is a natively embattled life, albeit an embattled life punctuated with 'joy unspeakable and full of glory'.

Third, we are to sharpen our *gospel focus*. When we do not feel forgiven, we must recall that our standing in Christ does not rest in anything in us (our feelings) or done by us (our works), but on the finished work of the Saviour upon the cross and on his continuing work at God's right hand as our great high priest. The Christian's whole comfort lies outside of himself. Perhaps this has nowhere been more memorably expressed than in the first question and answer of the *Heidelberg Catechism*:

> Q. 1. What is your only comfort in life and in death?

> A. That I, with body and with soul, both in life and in death, am not my own, but belong to my faithful Saviour Jesus Christ, who, with his precious blood, has fully satisfied for all my sins, and delivered me from all the power of the devil; and so preserves me, that without the will of my Father in heaven, not a hair can fall from my head; yea, that all things must work together for my salvation. Wherefore, by his Holy Spirit, he also assures me of eternal life, and makes me heartily willing and ready henceforth to live unto him.

God's truth and the grace of Christ are not qualified, far less nullified, by our feelings. However we might feel, however desperately wretched we might be, if we have believed in God's Son and are resting the whole weight of who we are on him alone, we are the most blessed and privileged of beings in the whole cosmos, whether we feel it to be so or not.

42. *Learning from Solomon:*
True and Needful Gospel Wisdom

Mention the name 'Solomon', and most Christians will immediately think of 'wisdom'. When Solomon began his kingship, the Lord appeared to him and said, 'Ask what I shall give you' (1 Kings 3:5). Solomon's reply 'pleased the Lord', because he asked, not for power and prestige, but for 'an understanding mind to govern your people' (1 Kings 3:9). Later, Solomon's wisdom had become so internationally known that the Queen of Sheba came to Jerusalem to find out for herself the wisdom of Solomon (1 Kings 10). If only Solomon's story had ended there! But it didn't.

The Bible, at times, can be deeply unsettling and make for very uncomfortable reading. Consider these opening verses of 1 Kings 11:

> Now King Solomon loved many foreign women, along with the daughter of Pharaoh: Moabite, Ammonite, Edomite, Sidonian, and Hittite women, from the nations concerning which the LORD had said to the people of Israel, 'You shall not enter into marriage with them, neither shall they with you, for surely they will turn away your heart after their gods.' Solomon clung to these in love. He had 700 wives, princesses, and 300 concubines.

And his wives turned away his heart. For when Solomon was old his wives turned away his heart after other gods, and his heart was not wholly true to the LORD his God, as was the heart of David his father. For Solomon went after Ashtoreth the goddess of the Sidonians, and after Milcom the abomination of the Ammonites. So Solomon did what was evil in the sight of the LORD and did not wholly follow the LORD, as David his father had done. Then Solomon built a high place for Chemosh the abomination of Moab, and for Molech the abomination of the Ammonites, on the mountain east of Jerusalem. And so he did for all his foreign wives, who made offerings and sacrificed to their gods (verses 1-8).

What have you thought as you read those words? 'How could he?' This is Solomon, whose reign began with such glowing promise; whom God so greatly commended because he did not ask him for wealth or power or fame, but rather for wisdom in order to rule God's covenant people justly and well. How could he? There are two answers, the obvious and the not so obvious.

First, he behaved as he did because he 'did what was evil in the sight of the LORD'. Solomon disobeyed God's clear commandment and did so again, and again, and again. There is always a price to pay when you disobey God. Solomon started (at least openly) his disobedience with Pharaoh's daughter, but it didn't end there. Sin and its unholy master, Satan, will always seek your complete downfall. They will never be content with making the occasional incursion into your life; they want to dominate and control your life. It is little wonder that Paul exhorted the church in Rome, 'if by the Spirit you put to death the deeds of the body, you will live' (Rom. 8:13). He understood the pathology and power of sin.

But there is a second answer that is not so obvious. Why did Solomon descend into such depths of sin? Why did Adam and Eve, so richly blessed by God and themselves without any sin, sin? Behold the mystery of iniquity! Yes, Solomon disobeyed God's clear command. But why did he do so? Why did he turn away from the God he knew, professed and served? Why did he abandon the God who had made him king? Behold the mystery of iniquity!

There is no rationality to sin. It is the ultimate absurdity. Who in their right mind would exchange the truth about God for a lie and worship and serve the creature rather than the Creator? (Rom. 1:25). But uncountable multitudes do. It is this note of irrational absurdity, and futility, that is reflected in the opening words of Psalm 2: 'Why do the nations rage and the peoples plot in vain?'

Why does God's word so graphically detail for us Solomon's tragic descent? To impress on us a truth that we desperately need to take to heart: 'The heart is deceitful above all things and desperately sick; who can understand it?' (Jer. 17:9). Solomon had every possible advantage in life but he descended into unimaginable wickedness. The application to you and to me is surely obvious: 'Let anyone who thinks that he stands take heed lest he fall' (1 Cor. 10:12). However blessed and spiritually privileged you have been to this moment, you are a step and a breath away from making shipwreck of your soul.

Perhaps you are thinking, 'Ian, are you not being a little too melodramatic?' I think not. The examples of Solomon and Demas (2 Tim. 4:10) confirm that I am not. Our Lord Jesus' teaching assures me that I am not (Mark 4:1-20). You are never as 'far along' as you think you are. 'Your adversary the devil prowls around like a roaring lion, seeking someone to devour' (1 Pet. 5:8).

Therefore, 'Watch and pray that you may not enter into temptation' (Matt. 26:41). Just as our Lord encouraged his hearers to 'Remember Lot's wife' (Luke 17:32), no less 'Remember Solomon's life', a life that began with such hope and promise but which descended into moral and spiritual tragedy.

The gospel life is therefore a wise life. It understands how vulnerable and weak the best of Christians are, even at their best. It is a life that watches and prays. It is a life that is always looking away to Jesus, the founder and perfector of faith (Heb. 12:2).

The gospel-shaped life is all about knowing Jesus, loving Jesus and living in moment-by-moment, heartfelt, prayerful dependence on Jesus. Jesus is the gospel-shaped life, its defining character and its supreme passion. Is your life a gospel-shaped life?

43. The Heart of Calvinism: Gospel Humility

Humility is a Christian grace. It is not native to any man or woman, no matter how quiet, peaceable, and inoffensive their temperament may be. So basic is humility to Christian faith and life that John Calvin, citing Augustine, comments on James 4:10 ('Humble yourselves before the Lord, and he will exalt you'):

> As a tree must strike deep roots downwards, that it may grow upwards, so everyone who has not his soul fixed deep in humility, exalts himself to his own ruin.

Many, of course, would be somewhat perplexed to find John Calvin of all people extolling the grace of humility. Is Calvinism not synonymous with pride and censoriousness? Was Calvin not a 'hard man'? Do the Calvinistic doctrines of election and predestination not inevitably breed pride, rather than humility? Not according to John Calvin! Without humility, he tells us, we exalt ourselves to our own ruin!

It can hardly be denied, however, that men claiming to be Calvinists have behaved arrogantly and censoriously, coldly and clinically. The problem is, in behaving like this they expose themselves as men who have no notion at all as to the true nature of what is called Calvinism. Benjamin

Warfield described Calvinism as 'that sight of the majesty of God that pervades all of life and all of experience'. What he meant is graphically pictured for us in the encounter that Isaiah had with the exalted Lord (Isa. 6:1ff.). That remarkable encounter did not leave Isaiah proud, superior, and censorious. How could it? On the contrary it 'undid' him. He cried, 'Woe to me! For I am lost ['undone', KJV]; for I am a man of unclean lips, and I dwell in the midst of a people of unclean lips; for my eyes have seen the King, the LORD of hosts!'

Here is the key that unlocks to us the true nature of authentic Calvinism. Calvinism can never be proud, cold, clinical and censorious, and that for one main reason: You cannot 'see the King' in his exalted majesty and have your sinful heart laid bare before him and still remain proud. This is precisely what Warfield meant when he said that the fountainhead of Calvinism does not lie in its theological system, but in its 'religious consciousness'. The roots of Calvinism are planted in a specific 'religious attitude', out of which springs (as day follows night) a particular theology. He wrote:

> The whole outworking of Calvinism in life is thus but the efflorescence of its fundamental religious consciousness, which finds its scientific statement in its theological system.[1]

---

[1] *Works*, V.354.

This is what so many miss in their assessment of, or espousal of, Calvinism. It is not first and foremost a theological system; it is more fundamentally a 'religious attitude', an attitude that gives inevitable birth to a particular, precise, but gloriously God-centred and heart-engaging system of theology. It needs to be said loudly, and often, that the 'formative principle' of Calvinism is not, then, what so many imagine, the doctrine of predestination, but the glory of the Lord God Almighty! The fundamental question posed in Calvinism is not, 'How can I be saved?', but 'How shall God be glorified?' Let me again quote Warfield:

> He who knows that it is God who has chosen him and not he who has chosen God, and that he owes his entire salvation in all its processes and in every one of its stages to this choice of God, would be an ingrate indeed if he gave not the glory of his salvation solely to the inexplicable elective love of God.[1]

It was this passionate conviction that lay behind the longing of David Brainerd for God's glory. In one of the last entries in his *Diary* he wrote:

> This day, I saw clearly that I should never be happy, yea, that God Himself could not make me happy, unless I could be in a capacity to 'please and glorify Him forever'. Take away this and admit me into all the fine havens that can be conceived of by men or angels, and I should still be miserable forever. ...

[1] *Works*, V.360.

> Oh, to love and praise God more, to please Him forever! This my soul panted after and even now pants for while I write. Oh, that God may be glorified in the whole earth.

Authentic Calvinism is natively meek-spirited. To claim to believe that God is the Sovereign King, that you owe all you are to his distinguishing grace and love, that you are and ever will be a 'debtor to mercy alone', while behaving proudly and treating other sinners, and even worse, Christian brothers, with supercilious disdain, is not to expose yourself as an inauthentic Calvinist, but to expose yourself as an inauthentic Christian!

Let me now take a step back.

Whenever men hear the word 'humility', notions of weakness and wetness almost inevitably spring into their minds. Who wants to be humble? Who wants to be likened to the obsequious Uriah Heep? Here, however, is the problem: Jesus Christ tells us that he himself is 'gentle and lowly in heart' (Matt. 11:28-30) and who more than he blazed against wickedness, hypocrisy and callousness? Who more than he evidenced authority in his words and acts? There was nothing of the spiritual '*invertebratus*' about our Saviour. Our Lord Jesus was the essence of the authentic Calvinist (if I can speak anachronistically). He learned in his humanity that salvation was his Father's sovereign prerogative: 'I thank you, Father, Lord of heaven and earth, that you have hidden these things from the wise and understanding and revealed them to little children; yes,

Father, for such was your gracious will' (Matt. 11:25-26). He believed that he would lose none of all that the Father had given to him (John 6:39). He knew that every event in history was ordained by his Father's will (see Matt. 10:29). Did this knowledge leave our blessed Saviour proud, distant, clinically dismissive of unenlightened sinners? Did he parade his 'Calvinism' for all to see? The very reverse was true. He was God's chosen Servant, his own dearly beloved Son. The Spirit was on him 'without limit'. And yet, indeed because of this, it was said of him, 'He will not quarrel or cry aloud, nor will anyone hear his voice in the streets; a bruised reed he will not break, and a smouldering wick he will not quench' (Matt. 12:18-20).

What difference, then, does Christlike humility produce in our lives? Much in every way! It will first inevitably pervade and shape how we approach God in worship. Whatever else marks Christian worship, a deep sense of the greatness and glory of God, and the littleness of man, will be a compelling note in our church gatherings. The shallowness and (sadly it has to be said) triviality that disfigures much that passes for worship today within evangelicalism would be exploded overnight, and dismissed overnight, if we were more deeply acquainted with the grace of humility. The admonition of the writer to the Hebrews would be our watchword: 'let us be grateful … and thus let us offer to God acceptable worship, with reverence and awe, for our God is a consuming fire' (Heb. 12:28-29). Please do not think for one moment that

I am advocating worship that is staid and dull—far from it. Worship that reverently exalts God and humbles man is instinct with life, the life of God's Spirit who delights to be present where Jesus, and not man, is the supreme focus of attention. Worship is not a performance where people admire and applaud the virtuoso skills of preacher, musicians, or whatever. Worship (as the word at its root means) is about bowing down, even prostrating ourselves, before the majesty of God's glory and grace.

Another evidence of true Christlike humility is preaching that depends on God's power and grace, not the preacher's ingenuity and personality. James Denney said, 'No man can give the impression that he himself is clever and that Christ is mighty to save.' Are you really persuaded that God, and God alone, can make an impact on sinners and saints alike with his gospel? Do you really believe that it is not of him who wills, or of him who runs, but of God who shows mercy? If you are a preacher, is all your preparation bathed in this unyielding conviction: 'Apart from God, I can do nothing'? Just as wisdom is justified of its children, so humility is seen in the spirit of childlike dependence. Too often, to my own shame, I have tried to be clever in the pulpit. It gives the impression of spirituality, but in truth it is the unmasking of a proud, unhumbled heart. Effective Christian living and preaching develops only in the soil of Christ-exalting, self-effacing humility. Well does God's word tell us that '"God opposes the proud but gives grace to the humble." Humble yourselves, therefore, under the mighty hand of God so that at the proper time he may exalt you' (1 Pet. 5:5-6).

Far from trampling on humility and promoting pride, authentic Calvinism by its very nature breeds a meek and lowly spirit. How can you or I be savingly united to the meek and lowly Saviour, and yet be proud, cold, and clinical in our Christianity? Proud Calvinism is the ultimate oxymoron.

Allow me, having said all this, to confess that Calvinism is indeed proud—it has got something to boast about. There can be no denying that Calvin, and his theological and spiritual heirs, were and are unapologetically proud. Our pride, however, is not in anything 'in us'. On the contrary we ought to be the first to confess that we are undeserving of the least of God's mercies, 'brands plucked from the burning', overwhelmed by the inexplicable wonder that 'the Son of God loved me and gave himself for me'. Where then does our pride lie? It lies exclusively in Jesus Christ alone. The boast of all authentic Calvinists is the same boast that echoed from Paul's soul: 'But far be it from me to boast except in the cross of our Lord Jesus Christ, by which the world has been crucified to me, and I to the world' (Gal. 6:14). Calvinism is proud, but only of the Saviour; proud of his glory and of his grace; proud that, though he was rich, yet for our poor, judgment-deserving sakes, he became poor, so that by his poverty we might become rich.

This is the mark of every gospel-shaped life.

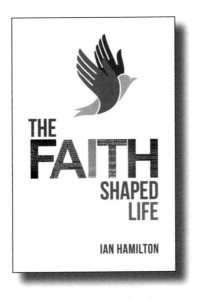

The Faith-Shaped Life
Ian Hamilton
160 pp. | paperback | ISBN: 978 1 84871 249 2
Also available as an ebook from
www.banneroftruth.org

*… a little gem, full of insight born of a deep biblical
understanding, an impressive grasp of the human
heart, and extensive pastoral experience.*

From a review by Peter Barnes.

The Banner of Truth Trust originated in 1957 in London. The founders believed that much of the best literature of historic Christianity had been allowed to fall into oblivion and that, under God, its recovery could well lead not only to a strengthening of the church, but to true revival.

Interdenominational in vision, this publishing work is now international, and our lists include a number of contemporary authors along with classics from the past. The translation of these books into many languages is encouraged.

A monthly magazine, *The Banner of Truth*, is also published. More information about this and all our publications can be found on our website or supplied by either of the offices below.

THE BANNER OF TRUTH TRUST

3 Murrayfield Road
Edinburgh, EH12 6EL
UK

PO Box 621, Carlisle
Pennsylvania 17013
USA

www.banneroftruth.org